A POCKET STYLE MANUAL

Third Edition

Clarity

Grammar

Punctuation and Mechanics

Research Sources

MLA, APA, *Chicago*

Usage/Grammatical Terms

Updated
with APA's
2001
guidelines

Diana Hacker

A Brief Contents

How to use this book

A Pocket Style Manual is a quick reference for writers and researchers. As a writer, you can turn to it for advice on revising sentences for clarity, grammar, punctuation, and mechanics. As a researcher, you can refer to its tips on finding and evaluating sources and to its color-coded sections on writing MLA, APA, and *Chicago*-style papers.

Here are the book's reference features.

The brief or detailed contents. The brief table of contents inside the front cover will usually send you close to the information you're looking for. Occasionally you may want to consult the more detailed contents inside the back cover.

The index. If you aren't sure which topic to choose in one of the tables of contents, turn to the index at the back of the book. For example, you may not realize that the choice between *is* and *are* is a matter of subject-verb agreement. In that case simply look up *"is* versus *are"* in the index and you will be directed to the pages you need.

Research sources. For advice on finding and evaluating sources both in the library and on the Internet, turn to sections 25 and 26.

MLA, APA, and* Chicago *papers. Color-coded sections—red for MLA, teal for APA, and blue for *Chicago*—keep you focused on the type of research paper your professor has assigned. Each section gives discipline-specific advice on supporting a thesis, avoiding plagiarism, and integrating and documenting sources. Directories to the documentation models are easy to find. Just look for the first of the pages marked with a band of the appropriate color: red, teal, or blue.

The glossaries. When in doubt about the correct use of commonly confused or misused words (such as *affect* and *effect*), consult section 43, the glossary of usage. To look up the meaning of a grammatical term, turn to section 44. There you will find brief definitions of terms such as *adjective, subordinate clause,* and *participial phrase.*

A Pocket Style Manual is meant to be consulted as the need arises. Keep it on your desk—right next to your dictionary—or tuck it into your backpack or jacket pocket and carry it with you as a ready resource.

A POCKET STYLE MANUAL

Third Edition

Clarity

Grammar

Punctuation and Mechanics

Research Sources

MLA, APA, *Chicago*

Usage / Grammatical Terms

Diana Hacker

Bedford / St. Martin's

Boston ◆ New York

For Bedford/St.Martin's
Developmental Editor: Leasa Burton
Production Editor: Anne Noonan
Production Supervisor: Joe Ford
Marketing Manager: Karen Melton
Copyeditor: Barbara G. Flanagan
Text Design: Claire Seng-Niemoeller
Cover Design: Hannus Design Associates
Composition: York Graphic Services
Printing and Binding: RR Donnelley and Sons Company

President: Charles H. Christensen
Editorial Director: Joan E. Feinberg
Director of Editing, Design, and Production: Marcia Cohen
Managing Editor: Elizabeth M. Schaaf

4   3   2   1
i   h   g

For information, write: Bedford/St. Martin's, 75 Arlington
Street, Boston, MA 02116
(617–399–4000)

ISBN: 0–312–40184–1

Acknowledgments

Lycos Search Web site: "Mountain Lion." (c) 1999 Lycos,
Inc. Lycos (tm) is a registered trademark of Carnegie
Mellon University. All rights reserved. Reprinted by
permission.

YAHOO! Web site. Text and artwork copyright (c) 1998
by *YAHOO!* Inc. All rights reserved. *YAHOO!* and the
YAHOO! logo are trademarks of *YAHOO!* Inc. Reprinted
by permission.

CLARITY

Clarity

Long sentences are not necessarily wordy, nor are short sentences always concise. A sentence is wordy if its meaning can be conveyed in fewer words.

1a. Redundancies

Redundancies such as *cooperate together, close proximity, basic essentials,* and *true fact* are a common source of wordiness. There is no need to say the same thing twice.

▶ Slaves were ~~portrayed or~~ stereotyped as lazy even

   though they were the main labor force of the

   South.

       works
▶ Daniel ~~is employed~~ at a rehabilitation center

   ~~working~~ as a physical therapist.

Modifiers are redundant when their meanings are suggested by other words in the sentence.

▶ Sylvia ~~very hurriedly~~ scribbled her name and

   phone number on the back of a greasy napkin.

1b. Empty or inflated phrases

An empty word or phrase can be cut with little or no loss of meaning. An inflated phrase can be reduced to a word or two.

▶ ~~The town of~~ New Harmony, ~~located in~~ Indiana, was

   founded as a utopian community.

                         if
▶ We will file the appropriate paper ~~in the event~~

   ~~that~~ we are unable to meet the deadline.

INFLATED	CONCISE
along the lines of	like
at the present time	now, currently
because of the fact that	because
by means of	by
due to the fact that	because
for the reason that	because
in order to	to
in spite of the fact that	although, though
in the event that	if
until such time as	until

1c. Needlessly complex structures

In a rough draft, sentence structures are often more complex than they need to be.

▶ ~~There is~~ *A*nother videotape ~~that~~ tells the story of

Charles Darwin and introduces the theory of

evolution.

▶ ~~It is imperative that~~ *A*ll police officers *must* follow strict

procedures when apprehending a suspect.

▶ The financial analyst claimed that because of

volatile market conditions she could not ~~make an~~

~~estimate of~~ the company's future profits.

2   Prefer active verbs.

As a rule, active verbs express meaning more vigorously than their duller counterparts—forms of the verb *be* or verbs in the passive voice. Forms of *be* (*be, am, is, are, was, were, being,* and *been*) lack vigor because they convey no action. Passive verbs lack strength because their subjects receive the action instead of doing it.

Although forms of *be* and passive verbs have legitimate uses, if an active verb can convey your meaning as well, use it.

FORM OF *BE*	A surge of power *was* responsible for the destruction of the coolant pumps.
PASSIVE	The coolant pumps *were destroyed* by a surge of power.
ACTIVE	A surge of power *destroyed* the coolant pumps.

2a. When to replace *be* verbs

Not every *be* verb needs replacing. The forms of *be* (*be, am, is, are, was, were, being, been*) work well when you want to link a subject to a noun that clearly renames it or to a vivid adjective that describes it: *Advertising is legalized lying. Great intellects are skeptical.*

If a *be* verb makes a sentence needlessly wordy, however, consider replacing it. Often a phrase following the verb will contain a word (such as *violation*) that suggests a more vigorous, active alternative (*violate*).

▶ Burying nuclear waste in Antarctica would ~~be in~~ *violate* ^ ~~violation of~~ an international treaty.

▶ When Rosa Parks ~~was resistant to~~ *resisted* ^ giving up her seat on the bus, she became a civil rights hero.

2b. When to replace passive verbs

In the active voice, the subject of the sentence does the action; in the passive, the subject receives the action.

| ACTIVE | The committee reached a decision. |
| PASSIVE | A decision was reached by the committee. |

In passive sentences, the actor (in this case *committee*) frequently disappears from the sentence: *A decision was reached.*

In most cases, you will want to emphasize the actor, so you should use the active voice. To replace a passive verb with an active alternative, make the actor the subject of the sentence.

Lightning struck the transformer,

► ~~The transformer was struck by lightning,~~
   ^

plunging us into darkness.

                           the doctor saw
► As the patient undressed, scars ~~were seen~~ on her
                              ^

back, stomach, and thighs.

The passive voice is appropriate when you wish to emphasize the receiver of the action or to minimize the importance of the actor. In the following sentence, for example, the writer wished to focus on the tobacco plants, not on the people spraying them: *As the time for harvest approachés, the tobacco plants are sprayed with a chemical to retard the growth of suckers.*

NOTE: In scientific writing, the passive voice properly puts the emphasis on the experiment or the process being described, not on the researcher: *The solution was heated to the boiling point, and then it was reduced in volume by 50 percent.*

3 Balance parallel ideas.

If two or more ideas are parallel, they should be expressed in parallel grammatical form.

A kiss can be a comma, a question mark, or an exclamation point.   —Mistinguett

This novel is not to be tossed lightly aside, but to be hurled with great force.   —Dorothy Parker

3a. Items in a series

Balance all items in a series by presenting them in parallel grammatical form.

▶ Cross-training involves a variety of exercises,
  lifting
such as running, swimming, and weights.
                                      ^

▶ The system has capabilities such as commun-

  icating with other computers, processing records,
      performing
and mathematical functions.
    ^

▶ In combat the soldiers were brave but sometimes

  foolish—because of poor training, lack of confi-
      inexperience.
dence, and ~~having little experience.~~
          ^

3b. Paired ideas

When pairing ideas, underscore their connection by
expressing them in similar grammatical form. Paired
ideas are usually connected in one of three ways:
(1) with a coordinating conjunction such as *and, but,* or
or; (2) with a pair of correlative conjunctions such as
either . . . or, neither . . . nor, not only . . . but also, or
whether . . . or; or (3) with a word introducing a com-
parison, usually *than* or *as.*

▶ Many states are reducing property taxes for home-
        extending
owners and ~~extend~~ financial aid in the form of tax
          ^
credits to renters.

The coordinating conjunction *and* connects two verbs:
reducing . . . extending.

▶ Thomas Edison was not only a prolific inventor but

also ~~was~~ a successful entrepreneur.

The correlative conjunctions *not only . . . but also* connect
two noun phrases: *a prolific inventor* and *a successful
entrepreneur.*

to ground

► It is easier to speak in abstractions than ~~grounding~~
                                   ^

one's thoughts in reality.

The comparative term *than* links two infinitive phrases: *to speak . . . to ground.*

---

4   Add needed words.

Do not omit words necessary for grammatical or logical completeness. Readers need to see at a glance how the parts of a sentence are connected.

4a. Words in compound structures

In compound structures, words are often omitted for economy: *Tom is a man who means what he says and [who] says what he means.* Such omissions are acceptable as long as the omitted word is common to both parts of the compound structure.

    If the shorter version defies grammar or idiom because an omitted word is not common to both parts of the structure, the word must be put back in.

► Some of the regulars are acquaintances whom we
                    who
see at work or live in our community.
            ^

The word *who* must be included because *whom live in our community* is not grammatically correct.

accepted

► Mayor Davis never has and never will accept a bribe.
                         ^

Has . . . accept is not grammatically correct.

in

► Tribes in the South Pacific still believe and live by
                                   ^

ancient laws.

Believe . . . by is not idiomatic English.

4b. The word *that*

Add the word *that* if there is any danger of misreading without it.

> *that*
> ▶ Many citizens do not believe the leaders of this
>   ⌃
>   administration are serious about reducing the
>
>   deficit.

Without *that,* readers might at first think that the citizens
don't believe the leaders.

4c. Words in comparisons

Comparisons should be between items that are alike. To
compare unlike items is illogical and distracting.

> *those of*
> ▶ Their starting salaries are higher than other
>   ⌃
>   professionals with more seniority.

Salaries must be compared with salaries, not with pro-
fessionals.

5   Eliminate confusing shifts.

5a. Shifts in point of view

The point of view of a piece of writing is the perspec-
tive from which it is written: first person (*I* or *we*), second person (*you*), or third person (*he/she/it/one* or *they*).
Writers who are having difficulty settling on an appropriate point of view sometimes shift confusingly from
one to another. The solution is to choose a suitable per-
spective and then stay with it.

> ▶ One week our class met to practice rescuing a
>   *We*
>   victim trapped in a wrecked car. ~~You~~ were graded
>   *our*   *our*   ⌃
>   on ~~your~~ speed and ~~your~~ skill.
>   ⌃   ⌃

You need
▶ ~~One needs~~ a password and a credit card number to
   ^

access this database. You will be billed at an

hourly rate.

Shifts from the third-person singular to the third-person plural are especially common.

Police officers are
▶ ~~A police officer is~~ often criticized for always being
   ^

there when they aren't needed and never being

there when they are.

Although the writer might have changed *they* to *he or she* (to match the singular *officer*), the revision in the plural is more concise. See pages 32–34.

NOTE: The *I* (or *we*) point of view, which emphasizes the writer, is a good choice for writing based primarily on personal experience. The *you* point of view, which emphasizes the reader, works well for giving advice or explaining how to do something. The third-person point of view, which emphasizes the subject, is appropriate in most academic and professional writing.

5b. Shifts in tense

Consistent verb tenses clearly establish the time of the actions being described. When a passage begins in one tense and then shifts without warning and for no reason to another, readers are distracted and confused.

▶ Rescue workers put water on her face and lifted
                                                  opened
   her head gently onto a pillow. Finally, she ~~opens~~
                                                  ^

her eyes.

Writers often shift verb tenses when writing about literature. The literary convention is to describe fictional events consistently in the present tense. (See pp. 30–31.)

▶ The scarlet letter is a punishment sternly placed

on Hester's breast by the community, and yet it ~~was~~
                                                  is
                                                   ^

an extremely fanciful and imaginative product of

Hester's own needlework.

6   Untangle mixed constructions.

A mixed construction contains parts that do not sensibly fit together. The mismatch may be a matter of grammar or of logic.

6a. Mixed grammar

A writer should not begin with one grammatical plan
and then switch without warning to another.

  M
▶ ~~For~~ ȷnost drivers who have a blood alcohol concen-

tration of .05 percent increase their risk of causing

an accident.

The phrase beginning with *For* cannot serve as the subject of the sentence. If the phrase opens the sentence, it
must be followed by a subject and a verb: *For most
drivers who have a blood alcohol concentration of .05 percent, the risk of causing an accident is increased.*

▶ Although the United States is one of the wealthi-

est nations in the world, ~~but~~ almost 20 percent of

American children live in poverty.

The *Although* clause is subordinate, so it cannot be linked
to an independent clause with the coordinating conjunction *but.*

6b. Illogical connections

A sentence's subject and verb should make sense together.

▶ Under the revised plan, the elderly/~~who now~~
                    the double personal exemption for
                    ∧
~~receive a double personal exemption~~/ will be

abolished.

The exemption, not the elderly, will be abolished.

▶ Social workers decided that ~~Tiffany's welfare~~ would
                             Tiffany
                             ∧
not be safe living with her mother.

Tiffany, not her welfare, may not be safe.

---

7 | Repair misplaced and dangling modifiers.

Modifiers should point clearly to the words they modify. As a rule, related words should be kept together.

7a. Misplaced words

The most commonly misplaced words are limiting modifiers such as *only, even, almost, nearly,* and *just.* They should appear in front of a verb only if they modify the verb: *At first I couldn't even touch my toes.* If they limit the meaning of some other word in the sentence, they should be placed in front of that word.

▶ Lasers ~~only~~ destroy the target, leaving the
         only
         ∧
surrounding healthy tissue intact.

The limiting modifier *not* is frequently misplaced, suggesting a meaning the writer did not intend.

▶ In 1860, all black southerners were ~~not~~ slaves.
       not
       ∧
The original sentence means that no black southerners were slaves. The revision makes the writer's real meaning clear.

7b. Misplaced phrases and clauses

Although phrases and clauses can appear at some distance from the words they modify, make sure your meaning is clear. When phrases or clauses are oddly placed, absurd misreadings can result.

▶ ~~There~~ are many pictures of comedians who have *On the walls*

performed at Gavin's . ~~on the walls.~~

The comedians weren't performing on the walls; the pictures were on the walls.

▶ The robber was described as a six-foot-tall man *150-pound,*

with a mustache . ~~weighing 150 pounds.~~

The robber, not the mustache, weighed 150 pounds.

7c. Dangling modifiers

A dangling modifier fails to refer logically to any word in the sentence. Dangling modifiers are usually introductory word groups that suggest but do not name an actor. When a sentence opens with such a modifier, readers expect the subject of the following clause to name the actor. If it doesn't, the modifier dangles.

DANGLING

Upon entering the doctor's office, a skeleton caught my attention.

This sentence suggests—absurdly—that the skeleton entered the doctor's office.

To repair a dangling modifier, you can revise the sentence in one of two ways:

1. Name the actor immediately following the introductory modifier, or
2. turn the modifier into a word group that names the actor.

▶ Upon entering the doctor's office, a skeleton . *I noticed*

~~caught my attention.~~

▶ *As I entered*
~~Upon entering~~ the doctor's office, a skeleton caught
　　^

my attention.

A dangling modifier cannot be repaired simply by moving it: *A skeleton caught my attention upon entering the doctor's office.* The sentence still suggests that the skeleton entered the doctor's office.

▶ *When the driver opened*
~~Opening~~ the window to let out a huge bumblebee,
　^

the car accidentally swerved into an oncoming car.

The car didn't open the window; the driver did. The writer has revised the sentence by mentioning the driver in the opening modifier.

▶ 　　　　　　　　　　　 *women have often been denied*
After completing seminary training, ~~woman's~~ access
　　　　　　　　　　　　　　　　　　　　^

to the pulpit▪ has ~~often been denied.~~
　　　　　　　 ^

The women (not their access to the pulpit) complete the training. The writer has revised the sentence by making *women* (not *women's access*) the subject.

7d. Split infinitives

An infinitive consists of *to* plus a verb: *to think, to dance.* When a modifier appears between its two parts, an infinitive is said to be "split": *to carefully balance.* If a split infinitive is awkward, move the modifier to another position in the sentence.

▶ The jurors were instructed to ~~very carefully~~ sift
　　　　　　　　　　　　　　　　 very carefully.
　through the evidence**/**
　　　　　　　　　 ^

When a split infinitive is more natural and less awkward than alternative phrasing, most readers find it acceptable. *We decided to actually enforce the law* is a perfectly natural construction in English. *We decided actually to enforce the law* is not.

8   Provide some variety.

When a rough draft is filled with too many same-sounding sentences, try to inject some variety—as long as you can do so without sacrificing clarity or ease of reading.

8a. Combining choppy sentences

If a series of short sentences sounds choppy, consider combining some of them. Look for opportunities to tuck some of your ideas into subordinate clauses. Subordinate clauses, which contain subjects and verbs, begin with words like these: *after, although, because, before, if, since, that, unless, until, when, where, which,* and *who.*

▶   The executive committee was made up of super-

      who

  stars/ ~~They~~ fought for leadership instead of

     ^

  addressing the company's problems.

▶   We keep our use of insecticides, herbicides, and

                   because we

  fungicides to a minimum/ ~~We~~ are concerned about

               ^

  the environment.

    Also look for opportunities to tuck some of your ideas into phrases, word groups that lack subjects or verbs (or both).

▶   The Chesapeake and Ohio Canal**,** ~~is~~ a 184-mile

                      ^

  waterway constructed in the 1800s**/** ~~It~~ was a major

                        ^

  source of transportation for goods during the

  Civil War.

   Noticing   *James*

▶   ~~James noticed~~ that the sky was glowing orange**/** He

  ^   ^

  bent down to crawl into the bunker.

At times it will make sense to combine short sentences by joining them with *and, but,* or *or.*

▶ Shore houses were flooded up to the first floor*/,*
    and

Brandt's Lighthouse was swallowed by the sea.

CAUTION: Avoid stringing a series of sentences together with *and, but,* or *or.* For sentence variety, place some of the ideas in subordinate clauses or phrases.

▶ ~~My~~ uncle noticed the frightened look on my face,
    When my

~~and~~ he told me that the dentures in the glass were

not real teeth.

▶ These particles*,* ~~are~~ known as "stealth liposomes,"

~~and they~~ can hide in the body for a long time

without detection.

8b. Varying sentence openings

Most sentences in English begin with the subject, move to the verb, and continue to an object, with modifiers tucked in along the way or put at the end. For the most part, such sentences are fine. Put too many of them in a row, however, and they become monotonous.

Words, phrases, or clauses modifying the verb can often be inserted ahead of the subject.

▶ A few drops of sap ~~eventually~~ began to trickle into
    Eventually a

the pail.

▶ ~~The~~ earthquake rumbled throughout the valley*.* ~~just~~
    Just as we were heading to work, the

~~as we were heading to work.~~

Participial phrases can frequently be moved to the beginning of a sentence without loss of clarity.

D
▶ ~~The university,~~ discouraged by the researchers'
^
the university
apparent lack of progress, nearly withdrew funding
^
for these prize-winning experiments.

NOTE: When you begin a sentence with a participial phrase, make sure that the subject of the sentence names the person or thing being described. If it doesn't, the phrase will dangle. (See 7c.)

9   Find an appropriate voice.

An appropriate voice is one that suits your subject, engages your audience, and conforms to the conventions of the genre in which you are writing. When in doubt about the conventions of a particular genre — lab reports, informal essays, research papers, business memos, and so on — look at models written by experts in the field.

In the academic, professional, and business worlds, three kinds of language are generally considered inappropriate: jargon, which sounds too pretentious; slang, which sounds too casual; and sexist or biased language, which offends many readers.

9a. Jargon

Jargon is specialized language used among members of a trade, profession, or group. Use jargon only when readers will be familiar with it; even then, use it only when plain English will not do as well.

JARGON   For many decades the indigenous body politic of South Africa attempted to negotiate legal enfranchisement without result.

REVISED   For many decades the indigenous people of South Africa negotiated in vain for the right to vote.

Broadly defined, jargon includes puffed-up language designed more to impress readers than to inform them. Common examples in business, government, higher education, and the military are given in the following list, with plain English translations in parentheses.

commence (begin)
components (parts)
endeavor (try)
exit (leave)
facilitate (help)
factor (consideration,
  cause)
finalize (finish)
impact (v.) (affect)

indicator (sign)
input (advice)
optimal (best)
parameters (boundaries)
prior to (before)
prioritize (set priorities)
utilize (use)
viable (workable)

    Sentences filled with jargon are hard to read, and they are often wordy as well.

▶ If managers ~~have adequate input from~~ *listen to* subordi-
nates, they can ~~effectuate more viable~~ *make better* decisions.

▶ All ~~employees functioning in the capacity of~~ work-
study students ~~are required to give evidence of~~ *must prove that they are currently enrolled.*
~~current enrollment.~~

9b. Slang

Slang is an informal and sometimes private vocabulary that expresses the solidarity of a group such as teenagers, rock musicians, or baseball fans. Although it does have a certain vitality, slang is a code that not everyone understands, and it is too informal for most written work.

▶ The government's "filth" guidelines will ~~gross~~ *disgust you.*
~~you out.~~

9c. Sexist language

Sexist language is language that stereotypes or demeans men or women, usually women. Such language arises from stereotypical thinking, from traditional pronoun use, and from words used to refer indefinitely to both sexes.

Stereotypical thinking.   In your writing, avoid referring to any one profession as exclusively male or exclusively female (such as referring to nurses in general as females). Also avoid using different conventions when identifying women and men (such as giving a woman's marital status but not a man's).

▶ All executives' ~~wives~~ *spouses* are invited to the picnic.

▶ Boris Stotsky, attorney, and ~~Mrs.~~ Cynthia Jones, *graphic designer,* ~~mother of three,~~ are running for city council.

The pronouns he *and* him.   Traditionally, *he, him,* and *his* were used to refer indefinitely to persons of either sex: *A journalist is stimulated by his deadline.* You can avoid such usage in one of three ways: substitute a pair of pronouns (*he or she, his or her*); reword in the plural; or revise the sentence to avoid the problem.

▶ A journalist is stimulated by his *or her* deadline.

▶ ~~A journalist is~~ *Journalists are* stimulated by ~~his deadline.~~ *their deadlines.*

▶ A journalist is stimulated by ~~his~~ *a* deadline.

Man words.   Like *he* and *his,* the nouns *man* and *men* and related words containing them were once used indefinitely to refer to persons of either sex. Use gender-neutral terms instead.

INAPPROPRIATE	APPROPRIATE
chairman	chairperson, chair
congressman	representative, legislator
fireman	firefighter
mailman	mail carrier, postal worker
mankind	people, humans
to man	to operate, to staff
weatherman	meteorologist, forecaster
workman	worker, laborer

9d. Offensive language

Obviously it is impolite to use offensive terms such as *Polack* or *redneck*, but offensive language can take more subtle forms. When describing groups of people, choose names that the groups currently use to describe themselves.

▶ North Dakota takes its name from the ~~Indian~~ *Sioux* word

meaning "friend" or "ally."

▶ Many ~~Oriental~~ *Asian* immigrants have recently settled in

our small town.

Avoid stereotyping a person or a group even if you believe your generalization to be positive.

▶ It was no surprise that Greer, ~~a Chinese American,~~ *an excellent math and science student,*

was selected for the honors chemistry program.

G
R
A
M
M
A
R

Grammar

10   Make subjects and verbs agree.

In the present tense, verbs agree with their subjects in number (singular or plural) and in person (first, second, or third). The present-tense ending *-s* is used on a verb if its subject is third-person singular; otherwise the verb takes no ending. Consider, for example, the present-tense forms of the verb *give*:

	SINGULAR	PLURAL
FIRST PERSON	I give	we give
SECOND PERSON	you give	you give
THIRD PERSON	he/she/it gives	they give
	Yolanda gives	parents give

The verb *be* varies from this pattern, and unlike any other verb it has special forms in *both* the present and the past tense.

PRESENT-TENSE FORMS OF *BE*		PAST-TENSE FORMS OF *BE*	
I am	we are	I was	we were
you are	you are	you were	you were
he/she/it is	they are	he/she/it was	they were

Problems with subject-verb agreement tend to arise in certain tricky contexts, which are detailed in this section.

10a. Words between subject and verb

Word groups often come between the subject and the verb. Such word groups, usually modifying the subject, may contain a noun that at first appears to be the subject. By mentally stripping away such modifiers, you can isolate the noun that is in fact the subject.

The *samples* on the tray in the lab *need* testing.

▶ High levels of air pollution damages the

respiratory tract.

The subject is *levels*, not *pollution*.

▶ The slaughter of pandas for their pelts ~~have~~ *has*

caused the panda population to decline drastically.

The subject is *slaughter*, not *pandas* or *pelts*.

NOTE: Phrases beginning with the prepositions *as well as*, *in addition to*, *accompanied by*, *together with*, and *along with* do not make a singular subject plural: *The governor, as well as his aide, was* [not *were*] *indicted*.

10b. Subjects joined by *and*

Compound subjects joined by *and* are nearly always plural.

▶ Jill's natural ability and her desire to help others ~~has~~ *have* led to a career in the ministry.

EXCEPTION: If the parts of the subject form a single unit, however, you may treat the subject as singular: *Bacon and eggs is my favorite breakfast*.

10c. Subjects joined by *or* or *nor*

With compound subjects connected by *or* or *nor*, make the verb agree with the part of the subject nearer to the verb.

▶ If a relative or neighbor ~~are~~ *is* abusing a child,

notify the police.

▶ Neither the lab assistant nor the students ~~was~~ *were* able

to download the program.

10d. Indefinite pronouns such as *someone*

Indefinite pronouns refer to nonspecific persons or things. Even though the following indefinite pronouns may seem to have plural meanings, treat them as singular in formal English: *anybody, anyone, each, either, everybody, everyone, everything, neither, none, no one, somebody, someone, something*.

> *favors*
> ▶ Nearly everyone on the panel ~~favor~~ the new budget.
>   ^

> *has*
> ▶ Each of the furrows ~~have~~ been seeded.
>   ^

A few indefinite pronouns (*all, any, some*) may be singular or plural depending on the noun or pronoun they refer to: *Some of the lemonade has disappeared. Some of the rocks were slippery.*

10e. Collective nouns such as *jury*

Collective nouns such as *jury, committee, club, audience, crowd, class, troop, family,* and *couple* name a class or a group. In American English, collective nouns are usually treated as singular: They emphasize the group as a unit.

> *meets*
> ▶ The board of trustees ~~meet~~ in Denver on the first
>   ^
> Tuesday of each month.

Occasionally, when there is some reason to draw attention to the individual members of the group, a collective noun may be treated as plural: *A young couple were arguing about politics while holding hands.* (Only individuals can argue and hold hands.)

NOTE: When units of measurement are used collectively, treat them as singular: *Three-fourths of the pie has been eaten.* When they refer to individual persons or things, treat them as plural: *One-fourth of the children were labeled "talented and gifted."*

10f. Subject after verb

Verbs ordinarily follow subjects. When this normal order is reversed, it is easy to become confused.

> *are*
> ▶ Of particular concern ~~is~~ penicillin and tetracycline,
>   ^
> antibiotics used to make animals more resistant
> to disease.

The subject *penicillin and tetracycline* is plural.

The subject always follows the verb in sentences beginning with *There is* or *There are* (or *There was* or *There were*).

▶ There ~~is~~ **are** a small aquarium and an enormous

terrarium in our biology lab.

The subject *aquarium and terrarium* is plural.

10g. *Who*, *which*, and *that*

Like most pronouns, the relative pronouns *who*, *which*, and *that* have antecedents, nouns or pronouns to which they refer. Relative pronouns used as subjects take verbs that agree with their antecedents.

Pick a stock that pays good dividends.

Problems arise with the constructions *one of the* and *only one of the*. As a rule, treat *one of the* constructions as plural, *only one of the* constructions as singular.

▶ Our ability to use language is one of the things
that ~~sets~~ **set** us apart from animals.

The antecedent of *that* is *things*, not *one*. Several things set us apart from animals.

▶ SEACON is the only one of our war games that
~~emphasize~~ **emphasizes** scientific and technical issues.

The antecedent of *that* is *one*, not *games*. Only one game emphasizes scientific and technical issues.

10h. Plural form, singular meaning

Words such as *athletics, economics, mathematics, physics, statistics, measles,* and *news* are usually singular, despite their plural form.

▶ Statistics ~~are~~ **is** among the most difficult courses in

our program.

EXCEPTION: When they describe separate items rather than a collective body of knowledge, words such as *athletics*, *mathematics*, and *statistics* are plural: *The statistics on school retention rates are impressive.*

10i. Titles, company names, and words mentioned as words

Titles, company names, and words mentioned as words are singular.

> *describes*
> ▶ *Lost Cities* ~~describe~~ the discoveries of many
>   ^
>
> ancient civilizations.

> *specializes*
> ▶ Delmonico Brothers ~~specialize~~ in organic produce
>   ^
>
> and additive-free meats.

> *is*
> ▶ *Controlled substances* ~~are~~ a euphemism for illegal
>   ^
>
> drugs.

---

11 | Be alert to other problems with verbs.

The verb is the heart of the sentence, so it is important to get it right. Section 10 deals with the problem of subject-verb agreement. This section describes a few other potential problems with verbs.

11a. Irregular verbs

For all regular verbs, the past-tense and past-participle forms are the same, ending in *-ed* or *-d*, so there is no danger of confusion. This is not true, however, for irregular verbs such as the following.

BASE FORM	PAST TENSE	PAST PARTICIPLE
begin	began	begun
fly	flew	flown
ride	rode	ridden

The past-tense form, which never has a helping verb, expresses action that occurred entirely in the past.

The past participle is used with a helping verb — either with *has, have,* or *had* to form one of the perfect tenses or with *be, am, is, are, was, were, being,* or *been* to form the passive voice.

PAST TENSE   Last July, we *went* to Paris.
PAST PARTICIPLE   We have *gone* to Paris twice.

When you aren't sure which verb form to choose (*went* or *gone, began* or *begun,* and so on), consult the list that begins on page 27. Choose the past-tense form if your sentence doesn't have a helping verb; choose the past-participle form if it does.

>   *saw*
> Yesterday we ~~seen~~ an unidentified flying object.
>   ^

> Because there is no helping verb, the past-tense form *saw* is required.

>   *fallen*
> By the end of the day, the stock market had ~~fell~~
>   ^
>
> two hundred points.

> Because of the helping verb *had,* the past-participle form *fallen* is required.

Distinguishing between lie *and* lay.   Writers often confuse the forms of *lie* (meaning "to recline or rest on a surface") and *lay* (meaning "to put or place something"). The intransitive verb *lie* does not take a direct object: *The tax forms are lying on the coffee table.* The transitive verb *lay* takes a direct object: *Please lay the tax forms on the coffee table.*

In addition to confusing the meanings of *lie* and *lay,* writers are often unfamiliar with the standard English forms of these verbs. Their past-tense and past-participle forms are given in the list of common irregular verbs that begins on page 27. The present participle of *lie* is *lying*; the present participle of *lay* is *laying*.

>   *lay*
> Elizabeth was so exhausted that she ~~laid~~ down
>   ^
>
> for a nap.

> The past-tense form of *lie* ("to recline") is *lay.*

> The prosecutor ~~lay~~ the pistol on a table close to
> ^laid^

the jurors.

The past-tense form of *lay* ("to place") is *laid*.

> Letters dating from the Civil War were ~~laying~~ in
> ^lying^

the corner of the chest.

The present participle of *lie* ("to rest on a surface") is
lying.

Common irregular verbs

BASE FORM	PAST TENSE	PAST PARTICIPLE
arise	arose	arisen
awake	awoke, awaked	awaked, awoke
be	was, were	been
beat	beat	beaten, beat
become	became	become
begin	began	begun
bend	bent	bent
bite	bit	bitten, bit
blow	blew	blown
break	broke	broken
bring	brought	brought
build	built	built
burst	burst	burst
buy	bought	bought
catch	caught	caught
choose	chose	chosen
cling	clung	clung
come	came	come
cost	cost	cost
deal	dealt	dealt
dig	dug	dug
dive	dived, dove	dived
do	did	done
drag	dragged	dragged
draw	drew	drawn
dream	dreamed, dreamt	dreamed, dreamt
drink	drank	drunk
drive	drove	driven
eat	ate	eaten
fall	fell	fallen
fight	fought	fought
find	found	found
fly	flew	flown

BASE FORM	PAST TENSE	PAST PARTICIPLE
forget	forgot	forgotten, forgot
freeze	froze	frozen
get	got	gotten, got
give	gave	given
go	went	gone
grow	grew	grown
hang (suspend)	hung	hung
hang (execute)	hanged	hanged
have	had	had
hear	heard	heard
hide	hid	hidden
hurt	hurt	hurt
keep	kept	kept
know	knew	known
lay (put)	laid	laid
lead	led	led
lend	lent	lent
let (allow)	let	let
lie (recline)	lay	lain
lose	lost	lost
make	made	made
prove	proved	proved, proven
read	read	read
ride	rode	ridden
ring	rang	rung
rise (get up)	rose	risen
run	ran	run
say	said	said
see	saw	seen
send	sent	sent
set (place)	set	set
shake	shook	shaken
shoot	shot	shot
shrink	shrank	shrunk, shrunken
sing	sang	sung
sink	sank	sunk
sit (be seated)	sat	sat
slay	slew	slain
sleep	slept	slept
speak	spoke	spoken
spin	spun	spun
spring	sprang	sprung
stand	stood	stood
steal	stole	stolen
sting	stung	stung
strike	struck	struck, stricken
swear	swore	sworn
swim	swam	swum
swing	swung	swung
take	took	taken

BASE FORM	PAST TENSE	PAST PARTICIPLE
teach	taught	taught
throw	threw	thrown
wake	woke, waked	waked, woken
wear	wore	worn
wring	wrung	wrung
write	wrote	written

11b. Tense

Tenses indicate the time of an action in relation to the time of the speaking or writing about that action. The most common problem with tenses — shifting from one tense to another — is discussed on pages 9–10. Other problems with tenses are detailed in this section, after the following survey of tenses.

Survey of tenses. Tenses are classified as present, past, and future, with simple, perfect, and progressive forms for each.

The simple tenses indicate relatively simple time relations. The present tense is used primarily for actions occurring at the time of the speaking or for actions occurring regularly. The past tense is used for actions completed in the past. The future tense is used for actions that will occur in the future. In the following table, the simple tenses are given for the regular verb *walk*, the irregular verb *ride*, and the highly irregular verb *be*.

PRESENT TENSE

SINGULAR		PLURAL	
I	walk, ride, am	we	walk, ride, are
you	walk, ride, are	you	walk, ride, are
he/she/it	walks, rides, is	they	walk, ride, are

PAST TENSE

SINGULAR		PLURAL	
I	walked, rode, was	we	walked, rode, were
you	walked, rode, were	you	walked, rode, were
he/she/it	walked, rode, was	they	walked, rode, were

FUTURE TENSE

I, you, he/she/it, we, they	will walk, ride, be

More complex time relations are indicated by the perfect tenses. A verb in one of the perfect tenses (a form of *have* plus the past participle) expresses an action that was or will be completed at the time of another action.

PRESENT PERFECT

| I, you, we, they | have walked, ridden, been |
| he/she/it | has walked, ridden, been |

PAST PERFECT

| I, you, he/she/it, we, they | had walked, ridden, been |

FUTURE PERFECT

| I, you, he/she/it, we, they | will have walked, ridden, been |

Each of the six tenses just mentioned has a progressive form used to express a continuing action. A progressive verb consists of a form of *be* followed by the present participle.

PRESENT PROGRESSIVE

I	am walking, riding, being
he/she/it	is walking, riding, being
you, we, they	are walking, riding, being

PAST PROGRESSIVE

| I, he/she/it | was walking, riding, being |
| you, we, they | were walking, riding, being |

FUTURE PROGRESSIVE

| I, you, he/she/it, we, they | will be walking, riding, being |

PRESENT PERFECT PROGRESSIVE

| I, you, we, they | have been walking, riding, being |
| he/she/it | has been walking, riding, being |

PAST PERFECT PROGRESSIVE

| I, you, he/she/it, we, they | had been walking, riding, being |

FUTURE PERFECT PROGRESSIVE

| I, you, he/she/it, we, they | will have been walking, riding, being |

Special uses of the present tense. Use the present tense when writing about literature or when expressing general truths.

is
▶ Don Quixote, in Cervantes's novel, ~~was~~ an idealist
  ^

  ill suited for life in the real world.

orbits
▶ Galileo taught that the earth ~~orbited~~ the sun.
  ^

The past perfect tense.   The past perfect tense is used for
an action already completed by the time of another past
action. This tense consists of a past participle preceded
by *had* (*had worked, had gone*).

▶ We built our cabin forty feet above an abandoned
  had been
  quarry that ~~was~~ flooded in 1920 to create a lake.
  ^

▶ When Hitler planned the Holocaust in 1941, did
  had
  he know that Himmler and the SS had mass
  ^

  murder in mind since 1938?

11c. Mood

There are three moods in English: the *indicative*, used
for facts, opinions, and questions; the *imperative*, used
for orders or advice; and the *subjunctive*, used for wishes,
conditions contrary to fact, and requests or recommendations. Of these three moods, the subjunctive is most
likely to cause problems.
   Use the subjunctive mood for wishes and in *if*
clauses expressing conditions contrary to fact. The subjunctive in such cases is the past tense form of the verb;
in the case of *be*, it is always *were* (not *was*), even if the
subject is singular.

   I wish that Jamal *drove* more slowly late at night.

   If I *were* a member of Congress, I would vote for the
   bill.

   Use the subjunctive mood in *that* clauses following
verbs such as *ask, insist, recommend,* and *request.* The
subjunctive in such cases is the base (or dictionary)
form of the verb.

Dr. Chung insists that her students *be* on time.

We recommend that Dawson *file* form 1050 soon.

11d. Voice

Transitive verbs (those that can take direct objects) appear in either the active or the passive voice. In the active voice, the subject of the sentence does the action; in the passive, the subject receives the action.

ACTIVE   John *hit* the ball.

PASSIVE   The ball was *hit* by John.

Because the active voice is simpler and more direct, it is usually more appropriate than the passive. (See section 2.)

12 Use pronouns with care.

Pronouns are words that substitute for nouns: *he, it, them, her, me,* and so on. Four frequently encountered problems with pronouns are discussed in this section:

a. pronoun-antecedent agreement (singular vs. plural)
b. pronoun reference (clarity)
c. case of personal pronouns (*I* vs. *me,* etc.)
d. *who* vs. *whom*

12a. Pronoun–antecedent agreement

The antecedent of a pronoun is the word the pronoun refers to. A pronoun and its antecedent agree when they are both singular or both plural.

SINGULAR   The *doctor* finished *her* rounds.

PLURAL   The *doctors* finished *their* rounds.

Writers are sometimes tempted to choose the plural pronoun *they* (or *their*) to refer to a singular antecedent. The temptation is greatest when the singular antecedent is an indefinite pronoun, a generic noun, or a collective noun.

Indefinite pronouns. Indefinite pronouns refer to non-specific persons or things. Even though some of the following indefinite pronouns may seem to have plural meanings, treat them as singular in formal English: *anybody, anyone, each, either, everybody, everyone, everything, neither, none, no one, someone, something.*

> In this class *everyone* performs at *his or her* [not *their*] fitness level.

When *they* or *their* refers mistakenly to a singular antecedent such as *everyone,* you will usually have three options for revision:

1. Replace *they* with *he or she* (or *their* with *his or her*).
2. Make the singular antecedent plural.
3. Rewrite the sentence.

Because the *he or she* construction is wordy, often the second or third revision strategy is more effective.

> *he or she is*
> ▶ When someone has been drinking, ~~they are~~ more
>
> likely to speed.

> *drivers have*
> ▶ When ~~someone has~~ been drinking, they are more
>
> likely to speed.

> *Someone who*   *is*
> ▶ ~~When someone~~ has been drinking/ ~~they are~~ more
>
> likely to speed.

NOTE: The traditional use of *he* (or *his*) to refer to persons of either sex is now widely considered sexist. (See p. 18.)

Generic nouns. A generic noun represents a typical member of a group, such as *a student,* or any member of a group, such as *any musician.* Although generic nouns may seem to have plural meanings, they are singular.

> Every *runner* must train rigorously if *he or she* wants [not *they want*] to excel.

When *they* or *their* refers mistakenly to a generic
noun, you will usually have the same three revision
options as for indefinite pronouns.

>   *he or she wants*
> ▶ A medical student must study hard if ~~they want~~ to
>   ^
>
>   succeed.

>   *Medical students*
> ▶ ~~A medical student~~ must study hard if they want to
>   ^
>
>   succeed.

> ▶ A medical student must study hard ~~if they want~~ to
>
>   succeed.

Collective nouns.   Collective nouns such as *jury, committee, audience, crowd, family,* and *team* name a class or
group. In American English, collective nouns are usually singular because they emphasize the group functioning as a unit.

>   The planning *committee* granted *its* [not *their*]
>   permission to build.

If the members of the group function individually,
however, you may treat the noun as plural: *The family
put their signatures on the document.* Or you might add
a plural antecedent such as *members* to the sentence:
*The members of the family put their signatures on the
document.*

12b. Pronoun reference

A pronoun should refer clearly to its antecedent. A pronoun's reference will be unclear if it is ambiguous, implied, vague, or indefinite.

Ambiguous reference.   Ambiguous reference occurs when
the pronoun could refer to two possible antecedents.

>   *it*   *the cake*
> ▶ When Aunt Harriet put ~~the cake~~ on the table, ~~it~~
>   ^   ^
>
>   collapsed.

> "*You have*"
► Tom told James, ~~that he had~~ won the lottery."

What collapsed—the cake or the table? Who won the lottery—Tom or James? The revisions eliminate the ambiguity.

Implied reference. A pronoun must refer to a specific antecedent, not to a word that is implied but not present in the sentence.

the braids
► After braiding Ann's hair, Sue decorated ~~them~~ with

ribbons.

Modifiers, such as possessives, cannot serve as antecedents. A modifier merely implies the noun that the pronoun might logically refer to.

Euripides
► In ~~Euripides'~~ *Medea*, ~~he~~ describes the plight of a

woman rejected by her husband.

Vague reference of this, that, *or* which. The pronouns *this*, *that*, and *which* should not refer vaguely to earlier word groups or ideas. These pronouns should refer to specific antecedents. When a pronoun's reference is too vague, either replace the pronoun with a noun or supply an antecedent to which the pronoun clearly refers.

► More and more often, especially in large cities, we

are finding ourselves victims of serious crimes. We
our fate
learn to accept ~~this~~ with minor complaints.

► Romeo and Juliet were both too young to have
a fact
acquired much wisdom, which accounts for

their rash actions.

Indefinite reference of they, it, *or* you. The pronoun *they* should refer to a specific antecedent. Do not use *they* to refer indefinitely to persons who have not been specifically mentioned.

       Congress
► ~~They~~ shut down all government agencies for more
    ^

than a month until the budget crisis was resolved.

The word *it* should not be used indefinitely in constructions such as "In the article it says that. . . ."

       The
► ~~In the~~ encyclopedia ~~it~~ states that male moths can
    ^

smell female moths from several miles away.

The pronoun *you* is appropriate when the writer is
addressing the reader directly: *Once you have kneaded
the dough, let it rise in a warm place*. Except in informal
contexts, however, the indefinite *you* (meaning "anyone
in general") is inappropriate.

       a person doesn't
► In Chad, ~~you don't~~ need much property to be
       ^

considered well-off.

12c. Case of personal pronouns (*I* versus *me*, etc.)

The personal pronouns in the following list change
what is known as case form according to their grammatical function in a sentence. Pronouns functioning
as subjects or subject complements appear in the *sub-
jective* case; those functioning as objects appear in the
objective case; and those functioning as possessives appear in the *possessive* case.

SUBJECTIVE CASE	OBJECTIVE CASE	POSSESSIVE CASE
I	me	my
we	us	our
you	you	your
he/she/it	him/her/it	his/her/its
they	them	their

For the most part, you know how to use these forms
correctly, but certain structures may tempt you to choose
the wrong pronoun.

Compound word groups. When a subject or object appears as part of a compound structure, you may occasionally become confused. To test for the correct pro-

noun, mentally strip away all of the compound structure except the pronoun in question.

▶ While diving for pearls, Ikiko and ~~her~~ found a

   she

   treasure chest full of gold bars.

> *Ikiko and she* is the subject of the verb *found*. Strip away the words *Ikiko and* to test for the correct pronoun: *she found* [not *her found*].

▶ The most traumatic experience for her father and
   ~~I~~ occurred long after her operation.

   me

> *Her father and me* is the object of the preposition *for*. Strip away the words *her father and* to test for the correct pronoun: *for me* [not *for I*].

Subject complements. Use subjective-case pronouns for subject complements, which rename or describe the subject and usually follow *be, am, is, are, was, were, being,* or *been.*

▶ During the Lindbergh trial, Bruno Hauptmann

   he.

   repeatedly denied that the kidnapper was ~~him~~.

> If *kidnapper was he* seems too stilted, rewrite the sentence: *During the Lindbergh trial, Bruno Hauptmann repeatedly denied that he was the kidnapper.*

Appositives. Appositives, noun phrases that rename nouns or pronouns, have the same function as the words they rename. To test for the correct pronoun, mentally strip away the words that the appositive renames.

   I,

▶ The chief strategists, Dr. Bell and ~~me,~~ could not

   agree on a plan.

> The appositive *Dr. Bell and I* renames the subject, *strategists*. Test: *I could not agree* [not *me could not agree*].

▶ The reporter interviewed only two witnesses, the

   me.

   shopkeeper and ~~I.~~

> The appositive *the shopkeeper and me* renames the direct object, *witnesses*. Test: *interviewed me* [not *interviewed I*].

We *or* **us** *before a noun.*   When deciding whether *we* or *us* should precede a noun, choose the pronoun that would be appropriate if the noun were omitted.

> *We*
> ▶ ~~Us~~ tenants would rather fight than move.
>   ^
>
>   Test: *We would rather fight* [not *Us would rather fight*].

>   *us*
> ▶ Management is short-changing ~~we~~ tenants.
>   ^
>
>   Test: *Management is short-changing us* [not *Management is short-changing we*].

Pronoun after **than** *or* **as.**   Sentence parts, usually verbs, are often omitted in comparisons beginning with *than* or *as*. To test for the correct pronoun, finish the sentence.

>   *I.*
> ▶ My husband is six years older than ~~me.~~
>   ^
>
>   Test: *than I* [*am*].

> ▶ We respected no other candidate in the election as
>   *her.*
>   much as ~~she.~~
>   ^
>
>   Test: *as* [*we respected*] *her.*

Pronoun before or after an infinitive.   An infinitive is the word *to* followed by a verb. Both subjects and objects of infinitives take the objective case.

>   *me*
> ▶ Ms. Wilson asked John and ~~I~~ to drive the senator
>   *her*   ^
>   and ~~she~~ to the airport.
>   ^
>
>   *John and me* is the subject and *senator and her* is the object of the infinitive *to drive*.

Pronoun or noun before a gerund.   If a pronoun modifies a gerund, use the possessive case: *my, our, your, his/her/its, their*. A gerund is a verb form ending in *-ing* that functions as a noun.

>   *your*
> ▶ The chances against ~~you~~ being hit by lightning
>   ^
>
>   are about two million to one.

Nouns as well as pronouns may modify gerunds. To form the possessive case of a noun, use an apostrophe and an -s (*a victim's suffering*) or just an apostrophe (*victims' suffering*). (See pp. 69–70.)

▶ The old order in France paid a high price for the
  aristocracy's
  ~~aristocracy~~ exploiting the lower classes.
  ^

12d. *Who* or *whom*

Who, a subjective-case pronoun, can be used only for subjects and subject complements. *Whom*, an objective-case pronoun, can be used only for objects. The words *who* and *whom* appear primarily in subordinate clauses or in questions.

In subordinate clauses.   When deciding whether to use *who* or *whom* in a subordinate clause, check for the word's function within the clause.

                       whoever
▶ He tells that story to ~~whomever~~ will listen.
                          ^

  Whoever is the subject of *will listen*. The entire subordinate clause *whoever will listen* is the object of the preposition *to*.

                                          whom
▶ You will work with our senior engineers, ~~who~~ you
                                            ^
  will meet later.

  Whom is the direct object of the verb *will meet*. This becomes clear if you restructure the clause: *you will meet whom later*.

In questions.   When deciding whether to use *who* or *whom* in a question, check for the word's function *within the question.*

  Who
▶ ~~Whom~~ was accused of receiving money from
  ^
  the Mafia?

  Who is the subject of the verb *was accused*.

▶ ~~Who~~ did the Democratic Party nominate in 1976?
  ^

> *Whom* is the direct object of the verb *did nominate*. This
> becomes clear if you restructure the question: *The Demo-*
> *cratic Party did nominate whom in 1976?*

13 Choose adjectives and adverbs with care.

Adjectives modify nouns or pronouns; adverbs modify
verbs, adjectives, or other adverbs.

Many adverbs are formed by adding *-ly* to adjectives (*formal, formally*). But don't assume that all words
ending in *-ly* are adverbs or that all adverbs end in *-ly*.
Some adjectives end in *-ly* (*lovely, friendly*) and some
adverbs don't (*always, here*). When in doubt, consult a
dictionary.

13a. Adverbs

Use adverbs, not adjectives, to modify verbs, adjectives,
and adverbs. Adverbs usually answer one of these questions: When? Where? How? Why? Under what conditions? How often? To what degree?

The incorrect use of adjectives in place of adverbs
to modify verbs occurs primarily in casual or nonstandard speech.

▶ The manager must see that the office runs
  smoothly   *efficiently.*
  ~~smooth~~ and ~~efficient.~~
  ^   ^

The incorrect use of the adjective *good* in place of
the adverb *well* is especially common in casual and nonstandard speech.

                                                well
▶ We were delighted that Nomo had done so ~~good~~
                                               ^

on the exam.

Adjectives are sometimes incorrectly used to modify adjectives or other adverbs.

▶ In the early 1970s, chances for survival of the bald

         really

eagle looked ~~real~~ slim.
    ^

13b. Adjectives

Adjectives ordinarily precede nouns, but they can also function as subject complements following linking verbs (usually a form of *be*: *be, am, is, are, was, were, being, been*). When an adjective functions as a subject complement, it describes the subject.

Justice is *blind*.

Problems can arise with verbs such as *smell, taste, look, appear, grow,* and *feel,* which may or may not be linking. If the word following one of these verbs describes the subject, use an adjective; if the word modifies the verb, use an adverb.

ADJECTIVE   The detective looked *cautious*.

ADVERB   The detective looked *cautiously* for the fingerprints.

Linking verbs usually suggest states of being, not actions. For example, to look cautious suggests the state of being cautious, whereas to look cautiously is to perform an action in a cautious way.

      good

▶ Lori looked ~~well~~ in her new raincoat.
      ^

                      bad

▶ All of us on the debate team felt ~~badly~~ about our
                      ^

performance.

The verbs *looked* and *felt* suggest states of being, not actions, so they should be followed by adjectives.

13c. Comparatives and superlatives

Most adjectives and adverbs have three forms: the positive, the comparative, and the superlative.

POSITIVE	COMPARATIVE	SUPERLATIVE
soft	softer	softest
fast	faster	fastest
careful	more careful	most careful
bad	worse	worst
good	better	best

Comparative versus superlative. Use the comparative to compare two things, the superlative to compare three or more.

▶ Which of these two brands of toothpaste is ~~best?~~ *better?*

▶ Hermos is the ~~more~~ *most* qualified of the three

applicants.

Form of comparatives and superlatives. To form comparatives and superlatives of most one- and two-syllable adjectives, use the endings *-er* and *-est: smooth, smoother, smoothest.* With longer adjectives, use *more* and *most* (or *less* and *least*): *exciting, more exciting, most exciting.*

Some one-syllable adverbs take the endings *-er* and *-est* (*fast, faster, fastest*), but longer adverbs and all of those ending in *-ly* use *more* and *most* (or *less* and *least*).

Double comparatives or superlatives. Do not use a double comparative (an *-er* ending and the word *more*) or a double superlative (an *-est* ending and the word *most*).

▶ All the polls indicated that Dewey was more ~~likelier~~ *likely* to win than Truman.

14 Repair sentence fragments.

As a rule, do not treat a piece of a sentence as if it were a sentence. To be a sentence, a word group must consist of at least one full independent clause. An independent clause has a subject and a verb, and it either stands alone as a sentence or could stand alone. Some fragments are clauses that contain a subject and a verb but begin with a subordinating word. Others are phrases that lack a subject, a verb, or both.

You can repair a fragment in one of two ways: Either pull the fragment into a nearby sentence, punctuating the new sentence correctly, or turn the fragment into a sentence.

14a. Fragmented clauses

A subordinate clause is patterned like a sentence, with both a subject and a verb, but it begins with a word that tells readers it cannot stand alone — a word such as _after, although, because, before, if, so that, that, though, unless, until, when, where, who,_ and _which._

Most fragmented clauses beg to be pulled into a sentence nearby.

▶ Patricia arrived on the island of Malta, ~~Where~~ _where_

   she was to spend the summer restoring frescoes.

If a fragmented clause cannot be gracefully combined with a nearby sentence, try rewriting it. The simplest way to turn a fragmented clause into a sentence is to delete the opening word or words that mark it as subordinate.

▶ Population increases and uncontrolled development

   are taking a deadly toll on the environment.
   _In_
   ~~So that in~~ many parts of the world, fragile

   ecosystems are collapsing.

14b. Fragmented phrases

Like subordinate clauses, certain phrases are sometimes mistaken for sentences. Frequently a fragmented phrase may simply be attached to a nearby sentence.

▶ The archaeologists worked slowly, ~~E~~_e_xamining and

   labeling every pottery shard they uncovered.

   The word group beginning with _Examining_ is a verbal phrase, not a sentence.

▶ Many adults suffer silently from agoraphobia. *A*
fear of the outside world.

A fear of the outside world is an appositive phrase, not a
sentence.

▶ It has been said that there are only three
indigenous American art forms: *J*azz, musical
comedy, and soap operas.

Clearly the list is not a sentence. Notice how easily a colon
corrects the problem. (See p. 67.)

If the fragmented phrase cannot be attached to a
nearby sentence, turn the phrase into a sentence. You
may need to add a subject, a verb, or both.

▶ If Eric doesn't get his way, he goes into a fit of rage.
he lies
For example, ~~lying~~ on the floor screaming or
opens *slams*
~~opening~~ the cabinet doors and then ~~slamming~~
them shut.

The writer corrected this fragment by adding a subject—
he—and substituting verbs for the verbals *lying, opening,*
and *slamming.*

14c. Acceptable fragments

Skilled writers occasionally use sentence fragments for
emphasis. In the following passage, Richard Rodriguez
uses a fragment (italicized) to draw attention to his
mother.

> Following the dramatic Americanization of their
> children, even my parents grew more publicly confi-
> dent. *Especially my mother.* She learned the names of
> all the people on our block.
>
> —*Hunger of Memory*

Although fragments are sometimes appropriate,
writers and readers do not always agree on when they
are appropriate. Therefore, you will find it safer to write
in complete sentences.

15 Revise run-on sentences.

Run-on sentences are independent clauses that have not been joined correctly. An independent clause is a word group that does or could stand alone as a sentence. When two or more independent clauses appear in one sentence, they must be joined in one of these ways:

— with a comma and a coordinating conjunction (_and, but, or, nor, for, so, yet_)

— with a semicolon (or occasionally a colon or a dash)

There are two types of run-on sentences. When a writer puts no mark of punctuation and no coordinating conjunction between independent clauses, the result is a fused sentence.

FUSED Gestures are a means of communication for everyone they are essential for the hearing-impaired.

A far more common type of run-on sentence is the comma splice — two or more independent clauses joined by a comma without a coordinating conjunction. In some comma splices, the comma appears alone.

COMMA Gestures are a means of communication for
SPLICE everyone, they are essential for the hearing-impaired.

In other comma splices, the comma is accompanied by a joining word that is _not_ a coordinating conjunction. There are only seven coordinating conjunctions in English: _and, but, or, nor, for, so, yet._

COMMA Gestures are a means of communication for
SPLICE everyone, however, they are essential for the hearing-impaired.

The word _however_ is a conjunctive adverb, not a coordinating conjunction. When a conjunctive adverb joins independent clauses, the clauses must be separated with a semicolon.

To correct a run-on sentence, you have four choices:

1. Use a comma and a coordinating conjunction.
2. Use a semicolon (or, if appropriate, a colon or a dash).
3. Make the clauses into separate sentences.
4. Restructure the sentence, perhaps by subordinating one of the clauses.

One of these revision techniques will usually work better than the others for a particular sentence. The fourth technique, the one requiring the most extensive revision, is frequently the most effective.

▶ Gestures are a means of communication for
but
everyone, they are essential for the hearing-
^
impaired.

▶ Gestures are a means of communication for
;
everyone/ they are essential for the hearing-
^
impaired.

▶ Gestures are a means of communication for
T
everyone/. they are essential for the hearing-
^
impaired.

Although gestures
▶ ~~Gestures~~ are a means of communication for
^
everyone, they are essential for the hearing-

impaired.

15a. Revision with a comma and a coordinating conjunction

When a coordinating conjunction (*and, but, or, nor, for, so, yet*) joins independent clauses, it is usually preceded by a comma.

▶ Most of his contemporaries had made plans for
but
their retirement, Tom had not.
^

15b. Revision with a semicolon (or a colon or a dash)

When the independent clauses are closely related and their relation is clear without a coordinating conjunction, a semicolon is an acceptable method of revision.

▶ Tragedy depicts the individual confronted with the

fact of death⸝ comedy depicts the adaptability and

ongoing survival of human society.

A semicolon is required between independent clauses that have been linked with a conjunctive adverb such as *however* or *therefore* or a transitional phrase such as *in fact* or *of course*. (See p. 65 for a more complete list.)

▶ The timber wolf looks like a large German

shepherd⸝; however, the wolf has longer legs,

larger feet, and a wider head.

If the first independent clause introduces a quoted sentence, use a colon.

▶ Carolyn Heilbrun has this to say about the future⸝:

"Today's shocks are tomorrow's conventions."

Either a colon or a dash may be appropriate when the second clause summarizes or explains the first. (See also 18b and 21d.)

▶ Nuclear waste is hazardous ~~this~~ ^:This^ is an

indisputable fact.

15c. Revision by separating sentences

If both independent clauses are long — or if one is a question and the other is not — consider making them separate sentences.

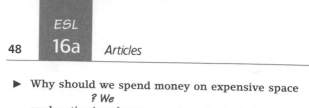

▶ Why should we spend money on expensive space

                        ? We

exploration/ ~~we~~ have enough underfunded
                ^

programs here on earth.

15d. Revision by restructuring the sentence

For sentence variety, consider restructuring the sentence, perhaps by turning one of the independent clauses into a subordinate clause or phrase.

   Although many
▶ ~~Many~~ scholars dismiss the abominable snowman
  ^

   of the Himalayas as a myth, others claim it may be

   a kind of ape.

▶ Nuclear power plants produce energy by fission,

   ~~it is~~ a process that generates radioactive waste.

---

16   If English is not your native language, check for common ESL problems.

This section of *A Pocket Style Manual* has a special audience: speakers of English as a second language (ESL) who have learned English but continue to have difficulty with a few troublesome features of the language.

16a. Articles

The definite article *the* and the indefinite articles *a* and *an* signal that a noun is about to appear. The noun may follow the article immediately or modifiers may intervene.

   the cat, the black *cat*
   a sunset, a spectacular *sunset*
   an apple, an appetizing *apple*

When to use a *(or* an*).*   Use *a* or *an* with singular count nouns whose specific identity is not known to the reader. Count nouns refer to persons, places, or things that can be counted: *one girl, two girls; one city, three cities*.

▶ Mary Beth arrived in *a* limousine.
^

▶ The biology student looked for *an* insect like the one
^

in his textbook.

A (or *an*) usually means "one among many" but can also mean "any one."

NOTE: *A* is used before a consonant sound: *a banana, a happy child. An* is used before a vowel sound: *an eggplant, an honorable person.* See the Glossary of Usage.

When not to use a *(or* an*).* *A* (or *an*) is not used to mark noncount nouns. Noncount nouns refer to entities or abstractions that cannot be counted: *water, silver, sugar, furniture, patience.* (See below for a fuller list.)

▶ Claudia asked her mother for ~~an~~ advice.

If you want to express an amount of something designated by a noncount noun, you can often add a quantifier in front of it: *a quart of milk, an ounce of gold, a piece of furniture.*

NOTE: A few noncount nouns may also be used as count nouns: *Bill loves lemonade; Bill offered me a lemonade.*

COMMONLY USED NONCOUNT NOUNS

Food and drink: bacon, beef, bread, broccoli, butter, cabbage, candy, cauliflower, celery, cereal, cheese, chicken, chocolate, coffee, corn, cream, fish, flour, fruit, ice cream, lemonade, lettuce, meat, milk, oil, pasta, rice, salt, spinach, sugar, tea, water, wine, yogurt

Nonfood substances: air, cement, coal, dirt, gasoline, gold, paper, petroleum, plastic, rain, silver, snow, soap, steel, wood, wool

Abstract nouns: advice, anger, beauty, confidence, courage, employment, fun, happiness, health, honesty, information, intelligence, knowledge, love, poverty, satisfaction, truth, wealth

Other: biology (and other areas of study), clothing, equipment, furniture, homework, jewelry, luggage, lum

ber, machinery, mail, money, news, poetry, pollution, research, scenery, traffic, transportation, violence, weather, work

When to use the.   Use the definite article *the* with most nouns whose specific identity is known to the reader. Usually the identity will be clear for one of these reasons:

1. The noun has been previously mentioned.
2. A word group following the noun restricts its identity.
3. The context or situation makes the noun's identity clear.

▶ A truck loaded with dynamite cut in front of our
                    the
  van. When truck skidded a few seconds later, we
             ^

  almost plowed into it.

The noun *truck* is preceded by *A* when it is first mentioned. When the noun is mentioned again, it is preceded by *the* since readers now know the specific truck being discussed.

                    the
▶ Bob warned me that gun on the top shelf of the
                   ^

  cupboard was loaded.

The phrase *on the top shelf of the cupboard* identifies the specific gun.

                  the
▶ Please don't slam door when you leave.
                  ^

Both the speaker and the listener know which door is meant.

When not to use the.   Do not use *the* with plural or non-count nouns meaning "all" or "in general."

    F
▶ ~~The~~ fountains are an expensive element of

  landscape design.

▶ In some parts of the world, ~~the~~ rice is preferred to

  all other grains.

Although there are many exceptions, do not use *the* with most singular proper nouns: names of persons (Jessica Webner); names of streets, squares, parks, cities, and states (Prospect Street, Union Square, Denali National Park, Miami, Idaho); names of continents and most countries (South America, Italy); and names of bays and single lakes, mountains, and islands (Tampa Bay, Lake Geneva, Mount Everest, Crete).

Exceptions to this rule include names of large regions, deserts, and peninsulas (the East Coast, the Sahara, the Iberian Peninsula) and names of oceans, seas, gulfs, canals, and rivers (the Pacific, the Dead Sea, the Persian Gulf, the Panama Canal, the Amazon).

NOTE: *The* is used to mark plural proper nouns: the United Nations, the Finger Lakes, the Andes, the Bahamas.

16b. Helping verbs and main verbs

Only certain combinations of helping verbs and main verbs make sense in English. The correct combinations are discussed in this section, after the following review of helping verbs and main verbs.

Review. Helping verbs always appear before main verbs.

HV MV   HV   MV
We *will leave* at noon. *Do* you *want* a ride?

Some helping verbs—*have, do,* and *be*—change form to indicate tenses; others, known as modals, do not.

FORMS OF *HAVE, DO,* AND *BE*

have, has, had
do, does, did
be, am, is, are, was, were, being, been

MODALS

can, could, may, might, must, shall, should, will, would (*also* ought to)

Every main verb has five forms (except *be*, which has eight). The following list shows these forms for the regular verb *help* and the irregular verb *give*. (See pp. 27–29 for a list of common irregular verbs.)

BASE FORM	help, give
-*S* FORM	helps, gives
PAST TENSE	helped, gave
PAST PARTICIPLE	helped, given
PRESENT PARTICIPLE	helping, giving

Modal + base form. After the modals *can, could, may, might, must, shall, should, will,* and *would,* use the base form of the verb.

▶ Geologists predicted that a minor earthquake

would occur~~s~~ along the Santa Ana fault line.

> *speak*
▶ We could ~~spoke~~ Spanish when we were young.
>   ^

Do, does, or *did + base form.* After helping verbs that are a form of *do,* use the base form of the verb.

▶ Mariko does not want~~s~~ any more dessert.

> *buy*
▶ Did Janice ~~bought~~ the gift for Katherine?
>   ^

Have, has, or *had + past participle.* To form one of the perfect tenses, use *have, has,* or *had* followed by a past participle (usually ending in *-ed, -d, -en, -n,* or *-t*). (See perfect tenses, pp. 29–31.)

> *offered*
▶ Many churches have ~~offer~~ shelter to the homeless.
>   ^

> *spoken*
▶ An-Mei has not ~~speaking~~ Chinese since she was a
>   ^

child.

Form of be *+ present participle.* To express an action in progress, use *am, is, are, was, were, be,* or *been* followed by a present participle (the *-ing* form of the verb).

> *turning*
▶ Because it is a clear night, I am ~~turn~~ my telescope
>   ^

to the constellation Cassiopeia.

> *driving*
> Uncle Roy was ~~driven~~ a brand-new red Corvette.
>   ^

The helping verbs *be* and *been* must be preceded by other helping verbs. See the progressive forms listed on page 30.

CAUTION: Certain verbs are not normally used in the progressive sense in English. In general, these verbs express a state of being or mental activity, not a dynamic action. Common examples are *appear, believe, have, hear, know, like, need, see, seem, taste, think, understand,* and *want.*

> *want*
> I ~~am wanting~~ to see August Wilson's *Seven Guitars*
>   ^
> at Arena Stage.

Form of be + *past participle.*   To form the passive voice, use *am, are, was, were, being, be,* or *been* followed by a past participle (usually ending in *-ed, -d, -en, -n,* or *-t*). When a sentence is written in the passive voice, the subject of the sentence receives the action instead of doing it. (See pp. 4–5.)

> *written*
> *Bleak House* was ~~write~~ by Charles Dickens.
>   ^
> *honored*
> The scientists were ~~honor~~ for their work with
>   ^
> endangered species.

In the passive voice, the helping verb *be* must be preceded by a modal: *Senator Dixon will be defeated. Being* must be preceded by *am, is, are, was,* or *were: The child was being teased. Been* must be preceded by *have, has,* or *had: I have been invited to a party.*

CAUTION: Although they may seem to have passive meanings, verbs such as *occur, happen, sleep, die,* and *fall* may not be used to form the passive voice because they are intransitive. Only transitive verbs, those that take direct objects, may be used to form the passive voice.

> The earthquake ~~was~~ occurred last Friday.

16c. Omitted subjects, expletives, or verbs

Some languages allow omission of subjects, expletives, or verbs in certain contexts. English does not.

English requires a subject for all sentences except imperatives, in which the subject *you* is understood (*Give to the poor*). If your native language allows the omission of an explicit subject, be especially alert to this requirement in English.

I have
▶ ~~Have~~ a large collection of baseball cards.
  ^

                                    he
▶ My brother is very bright; could read a book
                                  ^

before he started school.

When the subject has been moved from its normal position before the verb, English sometimes requires an expletive (*there* or *it*) at the beginning of the sentence or clause.

        there
▶ As you know, are many religious sects in India.
             ^

It is
▶ ~~Is~~ healthy to eat fruit and grains.
  ^

The subjects of these sentences are *sects* and *to eat fruit and grains*.

Although some languages allow the omission of the verb when the meaning is clear without it, English does not.

                              is
▶ Powell Street in San Francisco very steep.
                            ^

16d. Repeated subjects or objects

English does not allow a subject to be repeated in its own clause. This is true even if a word group intervenes between the subject and the verb.

▶ The painting that had been stolen ~~it~~ was found.

The pronoun *it* repeats the subject *painting*.

In some languages an object is repeated later in the adjective clause in which it appears; in English, such repetitions are not allowed. Adjective clauses usually begin with *who, whom, whose, which,* or *that,* and these words always serve a grammatical function within the clauses they introduce. Another word in the clause cannot also serve that same function.

▶ The puppy ran after the taxi that we were riding

in. ~~it.~~
  ^
The relative pronoun *that* is the object of the preposition *in,* so the object *it* is not allowed.

Even when the relative pronoun has been omitted, do not add another word with its same function.

▶ The puppy ran after the taxi we were riding in. ~~it.~~
                                                  ^
The relative pronoun *that* is understood.

PUNCTUATION

Punctuation

17 | The comma

The comma was invented to help readers. Without it, sentence parts can collide into one another unexpectedly, causing misreadings.

CONFUSING If you cook Elmer will do the dishes.

CONFUSING While we were eating a rattlesnake approached our campsite.

Add commas in the logical places (after *cook* and *eating*), and suddenly all is clear. No longer is Elmer being cooked, the rattlesnake being eaten.

Various rules have evolved to prevent such misreadings and to guide readers through complex grammatical structures. According to most experts, you should use a comma in the following situations.

17a. Before a coordinating conjunction joining independent clauses

When a coordinating conjunction connects two or more independent clauses — word groups that could stand alone as separate sentences — a comma must precede it. There are seven coordinating conjunctions in English: *and, but, or, nor, for, so,* and *yet.*

A comma tells readers that one independent clause has come to a close and that another is about to begin.

▶ Nearly everyone has heard of love at first sight,

but I fell in love at first dance.

EXCEPTION: If the two independent clauses are short and there is no danger of misreading, the comma may be omitted.

The plane took off and we were on our way.

CAUTION: Do *not* use a comma to separate compound elements that are not independent clauses. See page 63.

17b. After an introductory word group

Use a comma after an introductory clause or phrase. A comma tells readers that the introductory word group has come to a close and that the main part of the sentence is about to begin. The most common introductory word groups are adverb clauses, prepositional phrases, and participial phrases.

► When air-conditioning arrived in the workplace,
  it increased productivity significantly.

► Near a small stream at the bottom of the canyon,
  we discovered an abandoned shelter.

► Buried under layers of younger rocks, the earth's
  oldest rocks contain no fossils.

EXCEPTION: The comma may be omitted after a short clause or phrase if there is no danger of misreading.

In no time we were at 2,800 feet.

17c. Between items in a series

Use a comma between all items in a series, including the last two.

► Anne Frank and thousands like her were forced
  to hide in attics, cellars, and secret rooms.

Although some writers view the comma between the last two items as optional, most experts advise using it because its omission can result in ambiguity or misreading.

17d. Between coordinate adjectives

Use a comma between coordinate adjectives, those that each modify a noun separately.

► Patients with severe, irreversible brain damage
  should not be put on life support systems.

Adjectives are coordinate if they can be connected with *and*: *severe and irreversible.*

CAUTION: Do not use a comma between cumulative adjectives, those that do not each modify the noun separately.

> *Three large gray* shapes moved slowly toward us.

Adjectives are cumulative if they cannot be connected with *and*. It would be very odd to say *three and large and gray shapes*.

17e. To set off a nonrestrictive element

A *restrictive* element restricts the meaning of the word it modifies and is therefore essential to the meaning of the sentence. It is not set off with commas. A *nonrestrictive* element describes a word whose meaning already is clear. It is not essential to the meaning of the sentence and is set off with commas.

RESTRICTIVE

For camp the children needed clothes *that were washable*.

NONRESTRICTIVE

For camp the children needed sturdy shoes, *which were expensive*.

If you remove a restrictive element from a sentence, the meaning changes significantly, becoming more general than intended. The writer of the first sample sentence does not mean that the children needed clothes in general. The meaning is more restricted: The children needed *washable* clothes.

If you remove a nonrestrictive element from a sentence, the meaning does not change significantly. Some meaning is lost, to be sure, but the defining characteristics of the person or thing described remain the same as before. The children needed *sturdy shoes*, and these happened to be expensive.

Elements that may be restrictive or nonrestrictive include adjective clauses, adjective phrases, and appositives.

Adjective clauses.   Adjective clauses, which usually follow the noun or pronoun they describe, begin with a relative pronoun (*who, whom, whose, which, that*) or a relative adverb (*when, where*). When an adjective clause is nonrestrictive, set it off with commas; when it is restrictive, omit the commas.

NONRESTRICTIVE CLAUSE

▶ The United States Coast Survey, which was

   established in 1807, was the first scientific agency

   in this country.

RESTRICTIVE CLAUSE

▶ A corporation/that has government contracts/must

   maintain careful personnel records.

NOTE: Use *that* only with restrictive clauses. Many writers use *which* only with nonrestrictive clauses, but usage varies.

Adjective phrases.   Prepositional or verbal phrases functioning as adjectives may be restrictive or nonrestrictive. Nonrestrictive phrases are set off with commas; restrictive phrases are not.

NONRESTRICTIVE PHRASE

▶ The helicopter, with its 100,000-candlepower

   spotlight illuminating the area, circled above.

RESTRICTIVE PHRASE

▶ One corner of the attic was filled with newspapers/

   dating from the turn of the century.

Appositives.   An appositive is a noun or pronoun that renames a nearby noun. Nonrestrictive appositives are set off with commas; restrictive appositives are not.

NONRESTRICTIVE APPOSITIVE

▶ Darwin's most important book, *On the Origin of*

   Species, was the result of many years of research.

RESTRICTIVE APPOSITIVE

▶ The song⸍ "Fire It Up⸍" was blasted out of

amplifiers ten feet tall.

17f. To set off transitional and parenthetical expressions, absolute phrases, and contrasted elements

Transitional expressions. Transitional expressions serve as bridges between sentences or parts of sentences. They include conjunctive adverbs such as *however, therefore,* and *moreover* and transitional phrases such as *for example* and *as a matter of fact.* For a more complete list, see page 65.

When a transitional expression appears between independent clauses in a compound sentence, it is preceded by a semicolon and usually followed by a comma.

▶ Minh did not understand our language; moreover,
                                                ^
he was unfamiliar with our customs.

When a transitional expression appears at the beginning of a sentence or in the middle of an independent clause, it is usually set off with commas.

▶ As a matter of fact, nationalism is a relatively
                     ^
modern concept.

▶ Natural foods are not always salt free; celery, for
                                                ^
example, contains more sodium than most
       ^
people would imagine.

Parenthetical expressions. Expressions that are distinctly parenthetical, interrupting the flow of a sentence, should be set off with commas.

▶ Evolution, so far as we know, does not work this
           ^   ^
way.

Absolute phrases. An absolute phrase, which modifies the whole sentence, should be set off with commas.

▶ Our grant having been approved, we were at last

able to begin the archaeological dig.

Contrasted elements. Sharp contrasts beginning with words such as *not* and *unlike* are set off with commas.

▶ The Epicurean philosophers sought mental, not

bodily, pleasures.

17g. To set off nouns of direct address, the words *yes* and *no*, interrogative tags, and mild interjections

▶ Forgive us, Dr. Spock, for spanking Brian.
▶ Yes, the loan will probably be approved.
▶ The film was faithful to the book, wasn't it?
▶ Well, cases like this are difficult to decide.

17h. To set off direct quotations introduced with expressions such as *he said*

▶ Naturalist Arthur Cleveland Bent remarked, "In

part the peregrine declined unnoticed because it is

not adorable."

17i. With dates, addresses, titles

Dates. In dates, the year is set off from the rest of the sentence with commas.

▶ On December 12, 1890, orders were sent out for

the arrest of Sitting Bull.

EXCEPTIONS: Commas are not needed if the date is inverted or if only the month and year are given: *The deadline is 15 April 2001. May 1999 was a surprisingly cold month.*

Addresses. The elements of an address or place name are followed by commas. A zip code, however, is not preceded by a comma.

▶ Greg lived at 708 Spring Street, Washington,
  ^   ^

  Illinois 61571.

Titles. If a title follows a name, separate it from the rest of the sentence with a pair of commas.

▶ Sandra Barnes, M.D., performed the surgery.
               ^   ^

17j. Misuses of the comma

Do not use commas unless you have a good reason for using them. In particular, avoid using the comma in the following situations.

BETWEEN COMPOUND ELEMENTS THAT ARE NOT INDEPENDENT CLAUSES

▶ Marie Curie discovered radium/ and later applied

  her work on radioactivity to medicine.

TO SEPARATE A VERB FROM ITS SUBJECT

▶ Zoos large enough to give the animals freedom to

  roam/ are becoming more popular.

BETWEEN CUMULATIVE ADJECTIVES (See p. 59.)

▶ Joyce was wearing a slinky/ red silk gown.

TO SET OFF RESTRICTIVE ELEMENTS (See pp. 59–61.)

▶ Drivers/ who think they own the road/ make

  cycling a dangerous sport.

▶ Margaret Mead's book/ *Coming of Age in Samoa/* stirred up considerable controversy when it was first published.

AFTER A COORDINATING CONJUNCTION

▶ Occasionally soap operas are live, but/more often they are taped.

AFTER *SUCH AS* OR *LIKE*

▶ Plants such as/begonias and impatiens add color to a shady garden.

BEFORE *THAN*

▶ Touring Crete was more thrilling for us/than visiting the Greek islands frequented by the jet set.

BEFORE A PARENTHESIS

▶ At MCI Sylvia began at the bottom/ (with only a cubicle and a swivel chair), but within five years she had been promoted to supervisor.

TO SET OFF AN INDIRECT (REPORTED) QUOTATION

▶ Samuel Goldwyn once said/that a verbal contract isn't worth the paper it's written on.

WITH A QUESTION MARK OR AN EXCLAMATION POINT

▶ "Why don't you try it?/" she coaxed.

18 The semicolon and the colon

18a. The semicolon

The semicolon is used between independent clauses not joined by a coordinating conjunction. It can also be used between items in a series containing internal punctuation.

The semicolon is never used between elements of unequal grammatical rank.

Between independent clauses. When related independent clauses appear in one sentence, they are ordinarily connected with a comma and a coordinating conjunction (*and, but, or, nor, for, so, yet*). The coordinating conjunction expresses the relation between the clauses. If the relation is clear without a conjunction, a writer may choose to connect the clauses with a semicolon instead.

> Injustice is relatively easy to bear; what stings is justice. — H. L. Mencken

A writer may also choose to connect the clauses with a semicolon and a conjunctive adverb such as *however* or *therefore* or a transitional phrase such as *for example* or *in fact.*

> He swallowed a lot of wisdom; however, it seemed as if all of it had gone down the wrong way.
> — G. C. Lichtenberg

CONJUNCTIVE ADVERBS

accordingly, also, anyway, besides, certainly, consequently, conversely, finally, furthermore, hence, however, incidentally, indeed, instead, likewise, meanwhile, moreover, nevertheless, next, nonetheless, otherwise, similarly, specifically, still, subsequently, then, therefore, thus

TRANSITIONAL PHRASES

after all, as a matter of fact, as a result, at any rate, at the same time, even so, for example, for instance, in addition, in conclusion, in fact, in other words, in the first place, on the contrary, on the other hand

CAUTION: A semicolon must be used whenever a coordinating conjunction has been omitted between independent clauses. To use merely a comma—or to use a comma and a conjunctive adverb or transitional expression—creates an error known as a comma splice. (See pp. 45–48.)

▶ Some educators believe that African American history should be taught in separate courses; others prefer to see it integrated into survey courses.

▶ Many corals grow very gradually; in fact, the creation of a coral reef can take centuries.

Between items in a series containing internal punctuation. Ordinarily, items in a series are separated by commas. If one or more of the items contain internal punctuation, however, a writer may use semicolons instead.

> The only sensible ends of literature are first, the pleasurable toil of writing; second, the gratification of one's family and friends; and lastly, the solid cash.   — Nathaniel Hawthorne

Misuses of the semicolon.   Do not use a semicolon in the following situations.

BETWEEN AN INDEPENDENT AND A SUBORDINATE CLAUSE

▶ America has been called a country of pragmatists, although the American devotion to ideals is legendary.

BETWEEN AN APPOSITIVE AND THE WORD IT REFERS TO

▶ The scientists were fascinated by the species *Argyroneta aquatica,* a spider that lives underwater.

TO INTRODUCE A LIST

▶ Some of my favorite artists are featured on *Red, Hot, and Blue*: the Neville Brothers, Annie Lennox, and k. d. lang.

BETWEEN INDEPENDENT CLAUSES JOINED BY *AND, BUT, OR, NOR, FOR, SO,* OR *YET*

▶ Five of the applicants had worked with spreadsheets, but only one was familiar with database management.

18b. The colon

The colon is used after an independent clause to call attention to the words that follow it. The colon also has certain conventional uses.

Main uses of the colon.   After an independent clause, a writer may use a colon to direct the reader's attention to a list, an appositive, or a quotation.

A LIST

The routine includes the following: twenty knee bends, fifty leg lifts, and five minutes of running in place.

AN APPOSITIVE

There are only three seasons here: winter, July, and August.

A QUOTATION

Consider the words of John F. Kennedy: "Ask not what your country can do for you; ask what you can do for your country."

For other ways of introducing quotations, see pages 73–74.

A colon may also be used between independent clauses if the second summarizes or explains the first.

The Greeks were right: Character is fate.

The second clause may begin with a capital or a lowercase letter.

Minds are like parachutes: They [*or* they] function only when open.

Other uses.   Use a colon after the salutation in a formal letter, to indicate hours and minutes, to show proportions, between a title and subtitle, and to separate city and publisher in bibliographic entries.

Dear Sir or Madam:

5:30 P.M. (or p.m.)

The ratio of women to men was 2:1.

The Glory of Hera: Greek Mythology and the Greek Family

Boston: Bedford, 1997

NOTE: In biblical references, a colon is ordinarily used between chapter and verse (Luke 2:14). The Modern Language Association recommends a period (Luke 2.14).

Misuses of the colon.   A colon must be preceded by an independent clause. Therefore, avoid using it in the following situations.

BETWEEN A VERB AND ITS OBJECT OR COMPLEMENT

▶ Some important vitamins found in vegetables are̸ vitamin A, thiamine, niacin, and vitamin C.

BETWEEN A PREPOSITION AND ITS OBJECT

▶ The heart's two pumps each consist of̸ an upper chamber, or atrium, and a lower chamber, or ventricle.

AFTER *SUCH AS, INCLUDING,* OR *FOR EXAMPLE*

▶ The trees on campus include fine Japanese specimens such as̸ black pines, ginkgos, and cutleaf maples.

19   The apostrophe

The apostrophe is used to indicate possession and to mark contractions. In addition, it has a few conventional uses.

19a. To indicate possession

The apostrophe is used to indicate that a noun is possessive. Possessive nouns usually indicate ownership, as in *Tim's hat* or *the editor's desk*. Frequently, however, ownership is only loosely implied: *the tree's roots, a day's work*. If you are not sure whether a noun is possessive, try turning it into an *of* phrase: *the roots of the tree, the work of a day*.

When to add -'s.   Add -'s if the noun does not end in -s or if the noun is singular and ends in -s.

> A crocodile's life span is about thirteen years.

> Thank you for refunding the children's money.

> Lois's sister spent last year in India.

EXCEPTION: If pronunciation would be awkward with the added -'s, some writers use only the apostrophe: *Sophocles' plays are among my favorites.* Either use is acceptable.

When to add only an apostrophe.   If the noun is plural and ends in -s, add only an apostrophe.

> Both diplomats' briefcases were stolen.

Joint possession.   To show joint possession, use -'s (or -s') with the last noun only; to show individual possession, make all nouns possessive.

> Have you seen Joyce and Greg's new camper?

> Hernando's and Maria's expectations were quite different.

Compound nouns.   If a noun is compound, use -'s (or -s') with the last element.

> Her father-in-law's sculpture won first place.

Indefinite pronouns such as someone.   Use -'s to indicate that an indefinite pronoun is possessive. Indefinite pronouns refer to no specific person or thing: *everyone, someone, no one,* and so on.

> In a democracy, everyone's vote counts equally.

19b. To mark contractions

In a contraction, an apostrophe takes the place of missing letters.

> It's a shame that Frank can't go on the tour.

It's stands for *it is, can't* for *cannot.*
    The apostrophe is also used to mark the omission of the first two digits of a year (*the class of '99*) or years (*the '60s generation*).

19c. Conventional uses

Traditionally, an apostrophe has been used to pluralize numbers, letters, abbreviations, and words mentioned as words. The trend, however, is toward omitting the apostrophe.

Plural numbers.   Although an apostrophe was once used to pluralize numbers (figure 8's, the 1920's), the apostrophe is usually omitted in current usage.

> Peggy skated nearly perfect figure 8s.

> The 1920s are known as the Jazz Age.

Plural letters.   Current style manuals no longer recommend using an apostrophe to pluralize letters mentioned as letters. Italicize the letter and use roman type for the -*s* ending.

> Two large *J*s were painted on the door.

Plural abbreviations.   The trend is away from using an apostrophe to pluralize an abbreviation.

> We collected only four IOUs out of forty.

Plurals of words mentioned as words.   Current usage is to omit the apostrophe when the word mentioned as a word is italicized; notice that the *-s* ending appears in roman type.

> We've heard enough *maybe*s.

Words mentioned as words may also appear in quotation marks. When you choose this option, use the apostrophe.

> We've heard enough "maybe's."

19d. Misuses of the apostrophe

Do not use an apostrophe in the following situations.

WITH NOUNS THAT ARE NOT POSSESSIVE

outpatients
▶ Some ~~outpatient's~~ are given special parking
    ^

permits.

IN THE POSSESSIVE PRONOUNS *ITS, WHOSE, HIS, HERS, OURS, YOURS,* **AND** *THEIRS*

its
▶ Each area has ~~it's~~ own conference room.
    ^

It's means *it is.* The possessive pronoun *its* contains no apostrophe despite the fact that it is possessive.

20   Quotation marks

Quotation marks are used to enclose direct quotations. They are also used around some titles and to set off words used as words.

20a. To enclose direct quotations

Direct quotations of a person's words, whether spoken or written, must be in quotation marks.

> "A foolish consistency is the hobgoblin of little minds," wrote Ralph Waldo Emerson.

EXCEPTION: When a long quotation has been set off from the text by indenting, quotation marks are not needed. (See pp. 116, 151, and 161.)

Use single quotation marks to enclose a quotation within a quotation.

> According to Paul Eliott, Eskimo hunters "chant an ancient magic song to the seal they are after: 'Beast of the sea! Come and place yourself before me in the early morning!'"

20b. Around titles of short works

Use quotation marks around titles of newspaper and magazine articles, poems, short stories, songs, episodes of television and radio programs, and chapters or sub-divisions of books.

> The poem "Mother to Son" is by Langston Hughes.

NOTE: Titles of books, plays, and films and names of magazines and newspapers are put in italics or underlined. (See pp. 86–87.)

20c. To set off words used as words

Although words used as words are ordinarily under-lined to indicate italics (see p. 87), quotation marks are also acceptable.

> The words "affect" and "effect" are frequently confused.

20d. Other punctuation with quotation marks

This section describes the conventions to observe in placing various marks of punctuation inside or outside quotation marks. It also explains how to punctuate when introducing quoted material.

Periods and commas. Place periods and commas inside quotation marks.

> "This is a stick-up," said the well-dressed young couple. "We want all your money."

This rule applies to single and double quotation marks, and it applies to all uses of quotation marks.

NOTE: MLA and APA parenthetical citations are an exception to this rule. Put the parenthetical citation after the quotation mark and before the period. MLA: *Ac-*

cording to Cole, "The instruments of science have vastly extended our senses" (53). APA: *According to Cole (1999),"The instruments of science have vastly extended our senses" (p. 53).*

Colons and semicolons. Put colons and semicolons outside quotation marks.

> Harold wrote, "I regret that I cannot attend the AIDS fundraiser"; his letter, however, contained a contribution.

Question marks and exclamation points. Put question marks and exclamation points inside quotation marks unless they apply to the sentence as a whole.

> Contrary to tradition, bedtime at my house is marked by "Mommy, can I tell you a story now?"

> Have you heard the old proverb "Do not climb the hill until you reach it"?

In the first sentence, the question mark applies only to the quoted question. In the second sentence, the question mark applies to the whole sentence.

NOTE: MLA and APA parenthetical citations create a special problem. According to MLA and APA, the question mark or exclamation point should appear before the quotation mark, and a period should follow the parenthetical citation. MLA: *Esther Dyson asks, "How can the Net help education?" (101).* APA: *Esther Dyson (1998) has asked, "How can the Net help education?" (p. 101).*

Introducing quoted material. After a word group introducing a quotation, use a colon, a comma, or no punctuation at all, whichever is appropriate in context.

If a quotation has been formally introduced, a colon is appropriate. A formal introduction is a full independent clause, not just an expression such as *he said* or *she writes*.

> Morrow views personal ads as an art form: "The personal ad is like a haiku of self-celebration, a brief solo played on one's own horn."

If a quotation is introduced or followed by an expression such as *he said* or *she writes*, use a comma.

Stephen Leacock once said, "I am a great believer in luck, and I find the harder I work the more I have of it."

"You can be a little ungrammatical if you come from the right part of the country," writes Robert Frost.

When you blend a quotation into your own sentence, use either a comma or no punctuation, depending on the way in which the quotation fits into the sentence structure.

The future champion could, as he put it, "float like a butterfly and sting like a bee."

Hudson notes that the prisoners escaped "by squeezing through a tiny window eighteen feet above the floor of their cell."

If a quotation appears at the beginning of a sentence, set it off with a comma unless the quotation ends with a question mark or an exclamation point.

"We shot them like dogs," boasted Davy Crockett, who was among Jackson's troops.

"What is it?" I asked, bracing myself.

If a quoted sentence is interrupted by explanatory words, use commas to set off the explanatory words.

"A great many people think they are thinking," observed William James, "when they are merely rearranging their prejudices."

If two successive quoted sentences from the same source are interrupted by explanatory words, use a comma before the explanatory words and a period after them.

"I was a flop as a daily reporter," admitted E. B. White. "Every piece had to be a masterpiece — and before you knew it, Tuesday was Wednesday."

20e. Misuses of quotation marks

Do not use quotation marks to draw attention to familiar slang, to disown trite expressions, or to justify an attempt at humor.

▶ Between Thanksgiving and Super Bowl Sunday,

many American wives become/football widows./

Do not use quotation marks around indirect quotations. Indirect quotations report a person's words instead of quoting them directly.

▶ After leaving the scene of the domestic quarrel,

the officer said that/he was due for a coffee

break./

Do not use quotation marks around the title of your own essay.

21 Other marks

21a. The period

Use a period to end all sentences except direct questions or genuine exclamations. Use a period, not a question mark, for an indirect question — that is, a reported question.

Celia asked whether the picnic would be canceled.

A period is conventionally used with personal titles, Latin abbreviations, and designations of time.

Mr.	i.e.	A.M. (or a.m.)
Ms.	e.g.	P.M. (or p.m.)
Dr.	etc.	

A period is not used with postal service abbreviations for states, organization names, academic degrees, systems of chronology, and most capitalized abbreviations.

CA	NATO	PhD	BC
NY	AFL-CIO	RN	BCE
TX	IRS	BA	AD
USA (but U.S. when used as an adjective)	FCC	LLD	

Usage varies, however. When in doubt, consult a dictionary, a style manual, or a publication by the agency in question. Even the yellow pages can help.

NOTE: If a sentence ends with a period marking an abbreviation, do not add a second period.

21b. The question mark

Use a question mark after a direct question.

> What is the horsepower of a 747 engine?

If a polite request is written in the form of a question, you may use a question mark, though usage varies.

> Would you please send me your catalog of lilies?

CAUTION: Use a period, not a question mark, after an indirect question, one that is reported rather than asked directly.

> He asked me who was teaching the mythology course.

21c. The exclamation point

Use an exclamation point after a sentence that expresses exceptional feeling or deserves special emphasis.

> The medic shook me and kept yelling, "He's dead! He's dead! Can't you see that?"

CAUTION: Do not overuse the exclamation point.

▶ In the fisherman's memory the fish lives on,

increasing in length and weight with each passing

year, until at last it is big enough to shade a

fishing boat/.
          ^

This sentence doesn't need to be pumped up with an exclamation point. It is emphatic enough without it.

21d. The dash

The dash may be used to set off material that deserves special emphasis. When typing, use two hyphens to form a dash (--), with no spaces before or after them. (If your word processing program has what is known as an "em-dash," you may use it instead, with no space before or after it.)

Use a dash to introduce a list, a restatement, an amplification, or a dramatic shift in tone or thought.

> Along the wall are the bulk liquids — sesame seed oil, honey, safflower oil, and half-liquid peanut butter.

> Consider the amount of sugar in the average person's diet — 104 pounds per year.

> Kiere took a few steps back, came running full speed, kicked a mighty kick — and missed the ball.

In the first two examples, the writer could also use a colon. (See p. 67.) The colon is more formal than the dash and not quite as dramatic.

Use a pair of dashes to set off parenthetical material that deserves special emphasis or to set off an appositive that contains commas.

> Everything that went wrong — from the peeping Tom at her window to my head-on collision — was blamed on our move.

> In my hometown the basic needs of people — food, clothing, and shelter — are less costly than in Denver.

CAUTION: Unless you have a specific reason for using the dash, avoid it. Unnecessary dashes create a choppy effect.

▶ Seeing that our young people learn to use

computers makes good sense. Herding them ⧸

sheeplike ⧸ into computer technology does not.

21e. Parentheses

Use parentheses to enclose supplemental material, minor digressions, and afterthoughts.

> After taking her temperature, pulse, and blood pressure (routine vital signs), the nurse made Becky comfortable.

Use parentheses to enclose letters or numbers labeling items in a series.

> There are three points of etiquette in poker:
> (1) always allow someone to cut the cards,
> (2) don't forget to ante up, and (3) never stack
> your chips.

CAUTION: Do not overuse parentheses. Often a sentence reads more gracefully without them.

> *from ten to fifty million*
> ► Researchers have said that ~~ten million (estimates~~
>   ^
> ~~run as high as fifty million)~~ Americans have
>
> hypoglycemia.

21f. Brackets

Use brackets to enclose any words or phrases inserted into an otherwise word-for-word quotation.

> *Audubon* reports that "if there are not enough
> young to balance deaths, the end of the species
> [California condor] is inevitable."

The *Audubon* article did not contain the words *California condor* in the sentence quoted.

The Latin word "sic" in brackets indicates that an error in a quoted sentence appears in the original source.

> According to the review, Kistler's performance
> was brilliant, "exceding [sic] the expectations of
> even her most loyal fans."

21g. The ellipsis mark

Use an ellipsis mark, three spaced periods, to indicate that you have deleted material from an otherwise word-for-word quotation.

> Reuben reports that "when the amount of choles-
> terol circulating in the blood rises over . . . 300
> milligrams per 100, the chances of a heart attack
> increase dramatically."

If you delete a full sentence or more in the middle of a quoted passage, use a period before the three ellipsis dots.

NOTE: MLA now recommends putting brackets around ellipsis dots, like this: [. . .]. These brackets make clear that the ellipsis dots do not appear in the original work you are quoting (see pp. 115–116). You may wish to check with your instructor before following this new MLA guideline. If you are using a style other than MLA (such as APA), do not follow this guideline.

CAUTION: Do not use the ellipsis mark at the beginning of a quotation; do not use it at the end of a quotation unless you have cut some words from the end of the final sentence quoted.

21h. The slash

Use the slash to separate two or three lines of poetry that have been run in with your text. Add a space both before and after the slash.

> In the opening lines of "Jordan," George Herbert pokes gentle fun at popular poems of his time: "Who says that fictions only and false hair / Become a verse? Is there in truth no beauty?"

Use the slash sparingly, if at all, to separate options: *pass/fail, producer/director.* Put no space around the slash. Avoid using a slash for *he/she, and/or,* and *his/her.*

MECHANICS

Mechanics

22 Capitalization

In addition to the following guidelines, a good dictionary can often tell you when to use capital letters.

22a. Proper versus common nouns

Proper nouns and words derived from them are capitalized; common nouns are not. Proper nouns name specific persons, places, and things. All other nouns are common nouns.

The following types of words are usually capitalized: names for the deity, religions, religious followers, sacred books; words of family relationships used as names; particular places; nationalities and their languages, races, tribes; educational institutions, departments, degrees, particular courses; government departments, organizations, political parties; historical movements, periods, events, documents; specific electronic sources; and trade names.

PROPER NOUNS	COMMON NOUNS
God (used as a name)	a god
Book of Jeremiah	a sacred book
Grandmother Bishop	my grandmother
Father (used as a name)	my father
Lake Superior	a picturesque lake
the Capital Center	a center for advanced studies
the South	a southern state
Japan, a Japanese garden	an ornamental garden
University of Wisconsin	a good university
Geology 101	a geology course
Veterans Administration	a federal agency
Phi Kappa Psi	a fraternity
the Democratic Party	a political party
the Enlightenment	the eighteenth century
Great Depression	a recession
the Declaration of Independence	a treaty
the World Wide Web, the Web	a home page
the Internet, the Net	a computer network
Kleenex	a tissue

Months, holidays, and days of the week are capitalized: *May, Labor Day, Monday*. The seasons and numbers of the days of the month are not: *summer, the fifth of June*.

Names of school subjects are capitalized only if they are names of languages: *geology, history, English, French.* Names of particular courses are capitalized: *Geology 101, Principles of Economics.*

CAUTION: Do not capitalize common nouns to make them seem important: *Our company is currently hiring technical support staff* [not *Company, Technical Support Staff*].

22b. Titles with proper names

Capitalize titles of persons when used as part of a proper name but usually not when used alone.

> Prof. Margaret Burnes; Dr. Harold Stevens; John Scott Williams, Jr.; Anne Tilton, LLD.

> District Attorney Mill was ruled out of order.

> The district attorney was elected for a two-year term.

Usage varies when the title of an important public figure is used alone: *The president* [or *President*] *vetoed the bill.*

22c. Titles of works

In both titles and subtitles of works such as books, articles, and songs, major words should be capitalized. Minor words — articles, prepositions, and coordinating conjunctions — are not capitalized unless they are the first or last word of a title or subtitle. Capitalize the second part of a hyphenated term in a title only if it is a major word.

> *The Country of the Pointed Firs*

> *The Impossible Theater: A Manifesto*

> *The F-Plan Diet*

> "Fire and Ice"

> "I Want to Hold Your Hand"

> *The Canadian Green Page*

22d. First word of a sentence or quoted sentence

The first word of a sentence should of course be capitalized. Capitalize the first word of a quoted sentence but not a quoted phrase.

In *Time* magazine Robert Hughes writes, "There are only about sixty Watteau paintings on whose authenticity all experts agree."

Russell Baker has written that sports are "the opiate of the masses."

If a quoted sentence is interrupted by explanatory words, do not capitalize the first word after the interruption.

"When we all think alike," he said, "no one is thinking."

22e. First word following a colon

Do not capitalize the first word after a colon unless it begins an independent clause, in which case capitalization is optional.

There is one glaring omission in the Bill of Rights: the right to vote.

This we are forced to conclude: The [*or* the] federal government is needed to protect the rights of minorities.

22f. Abbreviations

Capitalize abbreviations for departments and agencies of government, other organizations, and corporations; capitalize trade names and the call letters of radio and television stations.

EPA, FBI, OPEC, IBM, Xerox, WCRB, KNBC-TV

23 Abbreviations, numbers, and italics (underlining)

23a. Abbreviations

Use abbreviations only when they are clearly appropriate.

Appropriate abbreviations.   Feel free to use standard abbreviations for titles immediately before and after proper names.

TITLES BEFORE PROPER NAMES	TITLES AFTER PROPER NAMES
Mr. Ralph Meyer	Thomas Hines, Jr.
Ms. Nancy Linehan	Anita Lor, PhD
Dr. Margaret Simmons	Robert Simkowski, MD
Rev. John Stone	William Lyons, MA
St. Joan of Arc	Margaret Chin, LLD
Prof. James Russo	Polly Stern, DDS

Do not abbreviate a title if it is not used with a proper name: *My history professor* [not *prof.*] *was an expert on naval warfare.*

Familiar abbreviations for the names of organizations, corporations, and countries are also acceptable.

CIA, FBI, AFL-CIO, NAACP, IBM, UPI, CBS, USA

The CIA was established in 1947 by the National Security Act.

When using an unfamiliar abbreviation (such as CBE for Council of Biology Editors) throughout a paper, write the full name followed by the abbreviation in parentheses at the first mention of the name. You may use the abbreviation alone from then on.

Other commonly accepted abbreviations include BC, AD, A.M., P.M., No., and $. The abbreviation BC ("before Christ") follows a date, and AD (*"anno Domini"*) precedes a date. Acceptable alternatives are BCE ("before the common era") and CE ("common era").

40 BC (or BCE)	4:00 A.M. (or a.m.)	No. 12 (or no. 12)
AD 44 (or CE)	6:00 P.M. (or p.m.)	$150

Do not use these abbreviations, however, when they are not accompanied by a specific figure: *We set off for the lake early in the morning* [not *A.M.*].

Inappropriate abbreviations. In formal writing, abbreviations for the following are not commonly accepted.

PERSONAL NAME   Charles [*not* Chas.]

UNITS OF MEASUREMENT   pound [*not* lb.]

DAYS OF THE WEEK   Monday [*not* Mon.]

HOLIDAYS   Christmas [*not* Xmas]

MONTHS   January, February, March [*not* Jan., Feb., Mar.]

COURSES OF STUDY   political science [*not* poli. sci.]

DIVISIONS OF WRITTEN WORKS   chapter, page [*not* ch., p.]

STATES AND COUNTRIES   Massachusetts [*not* MA or Mass.]

PARTS OF A BUSINESS NAME   Adams Lighting Company [*not* Adams Lighting Co.]; Kim and Brothers, Inc. [*not* Kim and Bros., Inc.]

Although Latin abbreviations are appropriate in footnotes and bibliographies and in informal writing, use the appropriate English phrases in formal writing.

cf. (Latin *confer,* "compare")

e.g. (Latin *exempli gratia,* "for example")

et al. (Latin *et alii,* "and others")

etc. (Latin *et cetera,* "and so forth")

i.e. (Latin *id est,* "that is")

N.B. (Latin *nota bene,* "note well")

23b. Numbers

Spell out numbers of one or two words. Use figures for numbers that require more than two words to spell out.

▶ The 1980 eruption of Mount St. Helens blasted

ash ~~12~~ *twelve* miles into the sky and devastated ~~two hundred thirty~~ *230* miles of land.

EXCEPTION: In technical and some business writing, figures are preferred even when spellings would be brief, but usage varies.

If a sentence begins with a number, spell out the number or rewrite the sentence.

▶ ~~150~~ *One hundred fifty* children in our program need expensive dental treatment.

Generally, figures are acceptable for the following.

DATES   July 4, 1776, 56 BC, AD 30

ADDRESSES   77 Latches Lane, 519 West 42nd Street

PERCENTAGES   55 percent (or 55%)

FRACTIONS, DECIMALS $\frac{1}{2}$, 0.047

SCORES   7 to 3, 21–18

STATISTICS   average age 37

SURVEYS   4 out of 5

EXACT AMOUNTS OF MONEY $105.37, $0.05

DIVISIONS OF BOOKS   volume 3, chapter 4, page 189

DIVISIONS OF PLAYS   Act I, scene i (or Act 1, scene 1)

IDENTIFICATION NUMBERS   serial no. 1098

TIME OF DAY   4:00 P.M., 1:30 A.M.

23c. Italics (underlining)

In handwritten or typed papers, underlining represents *italics,* a slanting typeface used in printed material.

Titles of works.   Titles of the following works are italicized or underlined.

TITLES OF BOOKS   *The Great Gatsby, A Distant Mirror*

MAGAZINES   *Time, Scientific American*

NEWSPAPERS   the *St. Louis Post-Dispatch*

PAMPHLETS   *Common Sense, Facts about Marijuana*

LONG POEMS   *The Waste Land, Paradise Lost*

PLAYS   *King Lear, A Raisin in the Sun*

FILMS   *The Truman Show, Casablanca*

TELEVISION PROGRAMS   *Frasier, 60 Minutes*

RADIO PROGRAMS   *All Things Considered*

MUSICAL COMPOSITIONS   Gershwin's *Porgy and Bess*

CHOREOGRAPHIC WORKS   Twyla Tharp's *Brief Fling*

WORKS OF VISUAL ART   Rodin's *The Thinker*

COMIC STRIPS   *Dilbert*

SOFTWARE   *WordPerfect*

WEB SITES   *Barron's Online*

The titles of other works, such as short stories, essays, songs, and short poems, are enclosed in quotation marks. (See p. 72.)

NOTE: Do not italicize or underline the Bible or the titles of books in the Bible (Genesis, not *Genesis*); the titles of legal documents (the Constitution, not the *Constitution*); or the titles of your own papers.

Names of ships, trains, aircraft, spacecraft. Italicize or underline names of specific ships, trains, aircraft, and spacecraft.

> *Challenger, Spirit of St. Louis, Queen Elizabeth II, Silver Streak*

▶ The success of the Soviets' Sputnik galvanized the U.S. space program.

Foreign words. Italicize or underline foreign words used in an English sentence.

▶ Instead of adhering to standard research protocol, I decided to establish my own modus operandi.

EXCEPTION: Do not italicize or underline foreign words that have become part of the English language — "laissez-faire," "fait accompli," "habeas corpus," and "per diem," for example.

Words as words, etc. Italicize or underline words used as words, letters mentioned as letters, and numbers mentioned as numbers.

▶ Tomás assured us that the chemicals could probably be safely mixed, but his probably stuck in our minds.

▶ Speakers of some dialects have trouble pronouncing the letter r.

▶ A big 3 was painted on the door to the lab.

NOTE: Quotation marks may be used instead of italics or underlining to set off words mentioned as words. (See p. 72.)

Inappropriate underlining. Underlining to emphasize words or ideas is distracting and should be used sparingly.

▶ Surfing the Internet can become an <u>addiction.</u>

24 Spelling and the hyphen

24a. Spelling

You learned to spell from repeated experience with words in both reading and writing. Words have a look, a sound, and even a feel to them as the hand moves across the page. As you proofread, you can probably tell if a word doesn't look quite right. In such cases, the solution is obvious: Look the word up in the dictionary.

A word processor equipped with a spell checker is a useful alternative to a dictionary, but only up to a point. A spell checker will not tell you how to spell words not listed in its dictionary; nor will it help you catch words commonly confused, such as *accept* and *except,* or common typographical errors, such as *own* for *won.* You will still need to proofread, and for some words you may need to turn to the dictionary.

NOTE: To check for correct use of commonly confused words (*accept* and *except, its* and *it's,* and so on), consult section 34, the Glossary of Usage.

Major spelling rules. If you need to improve your spelling, review the following rules and exceptions.

1. Use *i* before *e* except after *c* or when sounded like "ay," as in *neighbor* and *weigh.*

I BEFORE *E*	relieve, believe, sieve, niece, fierce, frieze
E BEFORE *I*	receive, deceive, sleigh, freight, eight
EXCEPTIONS	seize, either, weird, height, foreign, leisure

2. Generally, drop a final silent -*e* when adding a suffix that begins with a vowel. Keep the final -*e* if the suffix begins with a consonant.

desire, desiring   achieve, achievement

remove, removable   care, careful

Words such as *changeable, judgment, argument,* and *truly* are exceptions.

3. When adding -*s* or -*ed* to words ending in -*y,* ordinarily change -*y* to -*i* when the -*y* is preceded by a consonant but not when it is preceded by a vowel.

comedy, comedies   monkey, monkeys

dry, dried   play, played

With proper names ending in -*y,* however, do not change the -*y* to -*i* even if it is preceded by a consonant: *the Dougherty family, the Doughertys.*

4. If a final consonant is preceded by a single vowel *and* the consonant ends a one-syllable word or a stressed syllable, double the consonant when adding a suffix beginning with a vowel.

bet, betting   occur, occurrence

commit, committed

5. Add -*s* to form the plural of most nouns; add -*es* to singular nouns ending in -*s, -sh, -ch,* and -*x.*

table, tables   church, churches

paper, papers   dish, dishes

Ordinarily add -*s* to nouns ending in -*o* when the -*o* is preceded by a vowel. Add -*es* when it is preceded by a consonant.

radio, radios   hero, heroes

video, videos   tomato, tomatoes

To form the plural of a hyphenated compound word, add the -*s* to the chief word even if it does not appear at the end.

mother-in-law, mothers-in-law

NOTE: English words derived from other languages such as Latin or French sometimes form the plural as they would in their original language.

medium, media   chateau, chateaux

criterion, criteria

Spelling variations.   Following is a list of some common words spelled differently in American and British English. Consult a dictionary for others.

AMERICAN	BRITISH
canceled, traveled	cancelled, travelled
color, humor	colour, humour
judgment	judgement
check	cheque
realize, apologize	realise, apologise
defense	defence
anemia, anesthetic	anaemia, anaesthetic
theater, center	theatre, centre
fetus	foetus
mold, smolder	mould, smoulder
civilization	civilisation
connection, inflection	connexion, inflexion
licorice	liquorice

24b. The hyphen

In addition to the following guidelines, a dictionary will help you make decisions about hyphenation.

Compound words.   The dictionary will tell whether to treat a compound word as a hyphenated compound (*water-repellent*), one word (*waterproof*), or two words (*water table*). If the compound word is not in the dictionary, treat it as two words.

▶ The prosecutor chose not to cross-examine any
  ^
  witnesses.

▶ The poet kept a small note book on his nightstand
  so that he could record his dreams.

▶ Alice walked through the looking/glass into a
        ^

backward world.

Words functioning together as an adjective.   When two or
more words function together as an adjective before a
noun, connect them with a hyphen. Generally, do not
use a hyphen when such compounds follow the noun.

▶ Pat Hobbs is not yet a well-known candidate.
                              ^

▶ After our television campaign, Pat Hobbs will be

well/known.

Do not use a hyphen to connect *-ly* adverbs to the words
they modify.

▶ A slowly/moving truck tied up traffic.

NOTE: In a series, hyphens are suspended: *Do you prefer
first-, second-, or third-class tickets?*

Conventional uses.   Hyphenate the written form of fractions and of compound numbers from twenty-one to
ninety-nine. Also use the hyphen with the prefixes *all-,
ex-,* and *self-* and with the suffix *-elect.*

▶ One-fourth of my income goes for rent.
     ^
▶ The charity is funding more self-help projects.
                                        ^

Division of a word at the end of a line.   If a word must be
divided at the end of a line, use these guidelines:

1. Divide words between syllables.
2. Never divide one-syllable words.
3. Never divide a word so that a single letter stands
   alone at the end of a line or fewer than three letters begin a line.
4. When dividing a compound word at the end of a
   line, either make the break between the words that
   form the compound or put the whole word on the
   next line.

Division of an Internet address. To divide a long Internet address at the end of a line, do not insert a hyphen, because a hyphen could appear to be part of the address. If the address is mentioned in the text of your paper, divide it at some convenient point, such as after a slash or before a dot.

NOTE: When an Internet address appears in an MLA list of works cited, it must be divided after a slash. (See p. 132.)

RESEARCH

Research Sources

Before you begin researching your topic, consider what information you will need and where you are likely to find it. The following sources suggest a range of possibilities.

Research sources

LIBRARY SOURCES

—General and specialized reference works

—Books

—Articles in scholarly journals

—Articles in magazines and newspapers

—Government documents

—Primary sources such as diaries and letters

—Audiovisual materials

INTERNET SOURCES

—Web sites

—Reference works

—Electronic texts (books, poems, and so on)

—Government documents

—News articles

—Newsgroups and listservs

—MUD's and MOO's

—E-mail

FIELD RESEARCH

—Interviews

—Opinion surveys

—Discussion groups

—Literature from organizations

—Observations and experiments

Depending on your subject, some sources will prove more useful than others. For example, if your research question addresses a historical issue, you might look at reference works, books, scholarly articles, and primary sources such as speeches. If your research question addresses a current political issue, however, you might turn to magazine and newspaper articles, Web sites, government documents, Internet discussion groups, and possibly opinion surveys that you conduct yourself.

NOTE: A Bedford/St. Martin's Web site, *Research and Documentation Online,* lists many print and online sources, and it links directly to dozens of useful research sites. The Web address is <http://www.bedfordstmartins.com/hacker/resdoc>.

25a. Researching at the library

Most of the searching you do at the library will take place at computer terminals with specific functions. Some terminals are for accessing the computerized book catalog, others contain CD-ROM databases of periodicals, and still others serve as gateways to the Internet.

General and specialized reference works

For some topics, you may want to begin your search by consulting general or specialized reference works. Check with a reference librarian to see which works are available in electronic format.

General reference works include encyclopedias, biographical references, atlases, almanacs, and unabridged dictionaries. Many specialized reference works are available: *Encyclopedia of the Environment, Contemporary Artists, The Historical and Cultural Atlas of African Americans, Almanac of American Politics, Anchor Bible Dictionary,* and so on.

Books

Virtually all libraries use computer catalogs that allow you to search for books and often other materials—such as government documents and audiovisuals—at a computer terminal. While computer catalogs vary widely from library to library, most are easy to use, and a reference librarian will be available to help you if you get stuck. Most catalogs allow you to search for materials by subject, by author, or by title.

The most common type of searching is by subject. Searching the catalog by subject involves the use of keywords or subject headings, which prompt the computer to retrieve information about relevant books and other source materials. If your search results in too few or too many finds (or "hits"), try refining your search by using one of the techniques listed on page 99.

Once you have narrowed your search to a list of relevant sources, you can usually print out bibliographic information for a source, along with its call number. The call number is the book's address on the library shelf.

Periodicals

Periodicals are publications issued at regular intervals, such as magazines, newspapers, and scholarly or technical journals. To track down useful articles, consult a periodical index. Some of these indexes are in print form, but most are electronic databases. Both print and electronic indexes vary widely in format, subject, and coverage, so you may wish to check with a reference librarian to find the resources that best suit your needs.

You search for periodical articles in an electronic database just as you look for books in the library's computer catalog—by author, title, or subject keywords. (For advice on refining keyword searches, see p. 99.) Bibliographic records appear on the screen, and if further information is available (such as an abstract or the complete text), you can retrieve it by selecting the article you want.

CAUTION: Be careful not to confuse abstracts, which summarize articles, with actual articles.

Other library resources

Your library may have rare and unpublished manuscripts in a special collection. Holdings might also include government documents, records, tapes, and CD's; films and videos; and drawings, paintings, engravings, and slides.

If your research topic is especially complex or unusual, you may need greater resources than your library offers. In such a case, talk to a librarian about interlibrary loan, a process in which one library borrows materials from another.

25b. Researching on the Internet

Some of your research will probably take place on the Internet. This section describes several common strategies for locating relevant online sources.

CAUTION: Because the Internet lacks quality control, be sure to evaluate online sources with special care (see section 26).

Search engines

Millions of Internet sites are cataloged by search engines each day, so online searching can be a daunting process. To maximize your search efforts, consider your needs and the specialties of leading search engines such as these:

ALTA VISTA – <http://www.altavista.com>

Alta Vista is one of the most comprehensive search engines, so it is useful for finding obscure terms. This program allows you to restrict searches by date and by type of media—such as web pages, images, video, and audio.

EXCITE – <http://www.excite.com>

Excite is good at ranking the probable relevance of a site, and it suggests sites that are similar to ones you found helpful.

HOTBOT – <http://www.hotbot.com>

The opening page of *HotBot* lets you customize your search. For example, it allows you to specify date restrictions, type of media desired, and domain names.

INFOSEEK – <http://infoseek.go.com>

Infoseek allows you to conduct a search on the results of a previous search. It also lets you search for terms only in a particular field, such as titles or URL's.

LYCOS — <http://www.lycos.com>

Lycos maintains a directory and searchable database of its top 5 percent rated sites. *Lycos* allows you to conduct a search on the results of a previous search, and it offers advanced search features that let you set the relative importance of search parameters and choose the type of media desired.

YAHOO! — <http://www.yahoo.com>

Yahoo! has the most detailed subject directory of the leading search engines, so it is easy to click on a topic and see what's available. This program allows you to restrict a search by date.

SEARCHING BY CATEGORY Multilevel subject or topic directories arrange sites into manageable categories and allow you to find relevant sites without searching the entire Internet. (For an example, see the sample screen on this page.) Subject directories can be stand-alone programs such as *Argus Clearinghouse* <http://www .clearinghouse.net>, or they can be part of a search engine such as *Yahoo!* <http://www.yahoo.com>.

LIST OF CATEGORIES

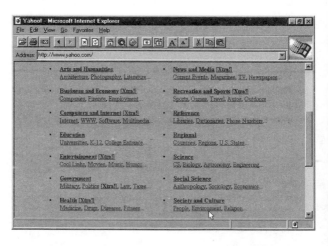

SEARCHING BY KEYWORD The amount of information returned by a simple keyword search, much of it irrelevant to your topic, can be overwhelming. To make the best use of your research time, spend a few minutes looking over the help screens in individual search engines.

Narrow or broaden your search as needed. Although not all search engines work in quite the same way, here are some of the most commonly used commands for narrowing or broadening your search.

— Use quotation marks around words that are part of a phrase: "Broadway musicals."

— Use AND to connect words that must appear in a document: Ireland AND peace. Some search engines require a plus sign instead: Ireland + peace.

— Use NOT in front of words that must not appear in a document: Titanic NOT movie. Some search engines require a minus sign instead: Titanic − movie.

— Use OR if only one of the words must appear in a document: "mountain lion" OR cougar.

— Use an asterisk as a substitute for letters that might vary: "marine biolog*".

— Use parentheses to group a search expression and combine it with another: (cigarettes OR tobacco OR smok*) AND lawsuits.

LIST OF HITS FROM A KEYWORD SEARCH

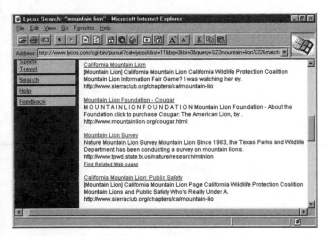

USING META SEARCH ENGINES   Meta search engines such as *Dogpile* <http://www.dogpile.com> and *Metacrawler* <http://www.metacrawler.com> search multiple search engines at once. Meta search engines are useful tools for conducting a preliminary search to determine what types of online sources are available.

Other online resources

Because they search the entire Web, search engines are likely to return a number of irrelevant hits and possibly bury relevant ones. To conduct a more focused search, turn to other online resources such as virtual libraries, text databases and archives, government sites, and news sites.

VIRTUAL LIBRARIES Virtual libraries are excellent resources for finding online references and useful research sites; some even offer advice on writing and documenting research papers. Virtual libraries are usually organized like subject directories, with hierarchical categories. For some especially useful virtual libraries such as *The Library of Congress* and *The Webliography,* consult the list on pages 217–218.

TEXT DATABASES AND ARCHIVES A number of useful online databases and archives house the complete texts of selected works such as poems, books, and speeches. The materials in these sites are usually limited to older works because of copyright laws. See page 218 for a list of impressive online collections.

GOVERNMENT SITES Many government agencies at every level provide online information services. Government-maintained sites include useful resources such as texts of laws, facts and statistics, government documents, and reference works. If your topic is a political issue, consider going to a site such as *U.S. Census Bureau: The Official Statistics* or *United Nations.* The URL's for these and other government sites are listed on page 218.

NEWS SITES Many popular newspapers, magazines, and television networks have online sites that offer some of the most up-to-date information available on the Web. These online services, such as *CNN Interactive* and *U.S. News Online,* often allow nonsubscribers or "guests" to search partial archives. See pages 218–19 for the URL's to these and other news sites.

Online communications

The Internet offers several communications options for conducting your own field research. You might join a listserv, for example, to send and receive e-mail messages relevant to your topic. Or you may wish to search a particular newsgroup's postings. See page 219 for sites that will lead you to listservs and newsgroups related to your topic.

In addition to listservs and newsgroups, you might log on to real-time discussion forums such as MUD's (multi-user dimensions) and MOO's (multi-user dimensions, object-oriented) to discuss your topic.

CAUTION: If you plan to use online communications to conduct field research, be aware that most of the people you contact will not be experts on your topic. Although you are more likely to find serious and worthwhile commentary in moderated listservs and scholarly discussion forums than in freewheeling newsgroups, it is difficult to guarantee the credibility of anyone you "meet" online.

26 Evaluating library and Internet sources

26a. Selecting sources worth your attention

As you conduct a library or Internet search, be alert for clues that indicate whether a book or article or Web site is worth tracking down. Titles often suggest the relevance of a source, and dates will help you rule out sources too old for consideration. In addition, many electronic indexes contain abstracts—brief summaries of articles—that can help you choose which articles to look at. Even the language used in a title or abstract can be a clue; the language might tell you, for example, that a source is too technical, too sensationalized, or not scholarly enough for your purposes.

Once you have tracked down a source, preview it quickly to see how much of your attention, if any, it is worth. Techniques for previewing a book, an article, and a Web site are a bit different.

PREVIEWING A BOOK

—Scan the front and back covers for any information about the book's scope and its author's credentials.

—Glance through the table of contents, keeping your research question in mind.

—Skim the preface in search of a statement of the author's purposes.

—Using the index, look up a few words related to your research question.

—If a chapter seems useful, read its opening and closing paragraphs and skim any headings.

—Consider the author's style and approach. Does the style suggest enough intellectual depth for your purposes? Does the author seem to present ideas in a balanced way?

PREVIEWING AN ARTICLE

—Consider the publication in which the article is printed. Is the publisher reputable? Who is the target audience of the publication? Might the publication be biased toward the target audience?

—For a magazine and journal article, look for an abstract or a statement of purpose at the beginning; also look for a summary at the end.

—For a newspaper article, focus on the headline and the opening sentences, known as the *lead*.

—Skim any headings and look at any charts, graphs, diagrams, or illustrations that might indicate the article's focus and scope.

PREVIEWING A WEB SITE

—Browse the home page. Do its contents and links seem relevant to your research question?

—Consider the reputation, credibility, and motive of the site's author. Consider also whether the sponsor might be biased in some way.

—Check to see when the site was last updated. For a current topic, some sites may be outdated.

26b. Distinguishing between primary and secondary sources

As you begin assessing the evidence in a text, consider whether you are reading a primary or a secondary source. Primary sources are original documents such as speeches, diaries, novels, legislative bills, laboratory studies, field research reports, and eyewitness accounts. Secondary sources are commentaries on primary sources.

Although a primary source is not necessarily more reliable than a secondary source, it has the advantage of being a firsthand account. Naturally, you can better evaluate what a secondary source says if you have first read any primary sources it discusses.

26c. Reading with an open mind and a critical eye

Both in print and online, some publishers and authors are more objective than others, so you will want to read your sources with a critical eye. The following checklists can guide your reading of both print and electronic sources.

CHECKING FOR SIGNS OF BIAS

— Do the author and publisher have reputations for accurate and balanced reporting?

— Does the author or publisher have political leanings or religious views that could affect objectivity?

— Is the author or publisher associated with a special-interest group, such as Greenpeace or the National Rifle Association, that might see only one side of an issue?

— How fairly does the author treat opposing views?

— Does the author's language show signs of bias?

ASSESSING AN ARGUMENT

— What is the author's central claim or thesis?

— How does the author support this claim — with relevant and sufficient evidence or with just a few anecdotes or emotional examples?

— Are the statistics accurate? Have they been used fairly? (It is possible to "lie" with statistics by using them selectively or by omitting mathematical details.)

—Are any of the author's assumptions questionable?

—Does the author consider opposing arguments and refute them persuasively?

—Does the author fall prey to any fallacies such as hasty generalizations or faulty cause-and-effect reasoning?

Because anyone can publish on the Web and because it is not always clear who authored or sponsored a site, you will need to be especially critical when judging the reliability of Web sources. Here are some questions to keep in mind:

—*Authorship.* Can you determine the author of the site? When you are on an internal page of a site, the author may not be named. To find out who wrote the material or what group sponsored the site, try going to the home page.

—*Credibility.* Is the author of the site knowledgeable and credible? Does the site offer links to the author's home page, résumé, or e-mail address?

—*Objectivity.* Who sponsors the site? Note that a site's domain name often specifies the type of group hosting the site: commercial (.com), educational (.edu), nonprofit (.org), governmental (.gov), or military (.mil).

—*Audience and purpose.* Who is the intended audience of the site? Why is the information available: to argue a position? to sell a product? to inform readers?

—*Documentation.* On the Internet, traditional methods of documentation are often replaced with links to original sources. Whenever possible, check out a linked source to confirm its authority.

—*Quality of presentation.* Consider the design and navigation of the site. Is it well laid out and easy to use? Do its links work, and are they up-to-date and relevant? Is the material well written and relatively free of errors?

M
L
A

MLA Papers

Most assignments in English and other humanities classes are based to some extent on reading. At times you will be asked to respond to one, two, or a few readings—such as essays or literary works. At other times you may be asked to write a research paper that draws on a wide variety of sources.

English and humanities instructors will usually ask you to document your sources with the Modern Language Association (MLA) system of citations described in section 31. When writing a paper that is based on sources, you face three main challenges: (1) supporting a thesis, (2) documenting your sources and avoiding plagiarism, and (3) integrating quotations and other source material.

27 Supporting a thesis

Most assignments ask you to form a thesis, or main idea, and to support that thesis with well-organized evidence.

27a. Finding a thesis

A thesis is a one-sentence (or occasionally a two-sentence) statement of your central idea. Usually your thesis will appear at the end of the first paragraph, but if you need to provide readers with considerable background information, you may place it at the end of the second paragraph, as in the example on page 140.

Although the thesis appears early in your paper, do not attempt to write it until fairly late in your reading and writing process. Reading and rereading will sharpen your ideas. And writing about a subject is a way of learning about it; as you write, your understanding of your subject will almost certainly deepen. As writer E. M. Forster once put it, "How can I know what I think until I see what I say?"

Early in the reading and writing process, you can keep your mind open — yet focused — by posing questions. The thesis that you articulate later in the process will be an answer to the central question you pose, as in the following examples.

PUBLIC POLICY QUESTION

Because of increasing numbers of mountain lion attacks on humans, should Californians reconsider their laws protecting the lions?

POSSIBLE THESIS

When Californians revisit the mountain lion question, they should frame the issue in a new way. A future proposition should retain the ban on sport hunting but allow the Department of Fish and Game to control the population.

LITERATURE QUESTION

In the classical Greek tragedy *Medea,* by Euripides, what is the central conflict: Is it within Medea's own heart (Should I kill my beloved children?) or is it between Medea and Jason, the man who has wronged her (How can I get revenge?)?

POSSIBLE THESIS

Medea professes great love for her children and seems torn between killing them and letting them live, but Euripides gives us reason to doubt her sincerity: Medea does not hesitate to use her children as weapons in her bloody battle with Jason, and from the outset she displays little real concern for their fate.

Notice that both thesis statements take a stand on a debatable issue — an issue about which intelligent, well-meaning people might disagree. Each writer's job will be to convince such people that his or her view is worth taking seriously.

27b. Organizing your evidence

The body of your paper will consist of evidence in support of your thesis. Instead of getting tangled up in details, organize this evidence in bold chunks—maybe three, four, or five chunks, each of which may turn out to be more than one paragraph long in your paper. In other words, keep your plan simple.

Perhaps the most common planning strategy is to list the key points in support of your thesis, as this student in a literature class has done.

—In three scenes Medea appears to be a loving mother, but in each scene we have reason to doubt her sincerity.

—Throughout the play, Medea's overriding concern is not her children but her reputation, her fear of ridicule, and her fame.

—After she kills her children, Medea shows no remorse and revels in Jason's agony over their death.

In the paper itself, the student was careful to begin each chunk of text with a topic sentence focusing the reader's attention on the topic about to be discussed. This was not difficult because she had already drafted such sentences when listing the key points of her paper.

It is not always necessary to use full sentences in your rough outline. For example, a student who wrote about the mountain lion problem in California used this simple list as his blueprint:

—The once endangered mountain lion

—Resurgence of the mountain lion

—Increasing attacks on humans

—The 1996 California referendum

—Population control: a reasonable solution

To make the organization of his paper clear to readers, this student used these phrases as headings in his paper, a technique often used in academic journals.

28 Citing sources; avoiding plagiarism

In researched writing, you will be drawing on the work of other writers, and you must document their contributions by citing your sources. Sources are cited for two reasons: to tell readers where your information comes from and to give credit to the writers from whom you have borrowed words and ideas. To borrow another writer's language or ideas without proper acknowledgment is a form of dishonesty known as *plagiarism*.

28a. Citing sources

Citations are required when you quote from a source, when you summarize or paraphrase a source, and when you borrow facts and ideas from a source (except for common knowledge). Here, very briefly, is how the MLA citation system usually works. See section 31 for a detailed discussion of variations.

1. The source is introduced by a signal phrase that names its author.
2. The material being cited is followed by a page number in parentheses.
3. At the end of the paper, a list of works cited (arranged alphabetically according to the authors' last names) gives complete publication information about the source.

IN-TEXT CITATION

As lion authority John Seidensticker remarks, "The boldness displayed by mountain lions just doesn't square with the shy, retiring behavior familiar to those of us who have studied these animals" (117).

ENTRY IN THE LIST OF WORKS CITED

Seidensticker, John. "Mountain Lions Don't Stalk People: True or False?" Audubon Feb. 1992: 113-22.

28b. Avoiding plagiarism

Your research paper is a collaboration between you and
your sources. To be fair and ethical, you must acknowledge
your debt to the writers of these sources. If you don't, you
are guilty of plagiarism, a serious academic offense.

Three different acts are considered plagiarism: (1)
failing to cite quotations and borrowed ideas, (2) failing
to enclose borrowed language in quotation marks, and
(3) failing to put summaries and paraphrases in your
own words.

Citing quotations and borrowed ideas.   You must of course
document all direct quotations. You must also cite any
ideas borrowed from a source: paraphrases of sentences,
summaries of paragraphs or chapters, statistics and
little-known facts, and tables, graphs, or diagrams.

The only exception is common knowledge—information that your readers could find in any number of
general sources because it is commonly known. For example, it is commonly known that Toni Morrison won
the Nobel Prize for literature in 1993 and that during
her lifetime Emily Dickinson published only a handful
of her many poems.

As a rule, when you have seen certain information
repeatedly in your reading, you don't need to cite it.
However, when information has appeared in only one
or two sources or when it is controversial, you should
cite it. If a topic is new to you and you are not sure what
is considered common knowledge or what is controversial, ask someone with expertise. When in doubt, cite the
source.

Enclosing borrowed language in quotation marks.   To indicate
that you are using a source's exact phrases or sentences, you must enclose them in quotation marks
unless they have been set off from the text by indenting. (See pp. 116–17 and 120–22.) To omit the quotation marks is to claim—falsely—that the language is
your own. Such an omission is plagiarism even if you
have cited the source.

ORIGINAL SOURCE

We see conflicting pictures of the mountain lion
through the eyes of hunters, ranchers, scientists,

wildlife managers, and preservationists. Each
viewpoint, like a piece of glass in a kaleidoscope, is a
shard, a fragment until it is combined with the other
pieces to create a total image.
— Karen McCall and Jim Dutcher, *Cougar: Ghost of
the Rockies,* p. 137

PLAGIARISM

McCall and Dutcher observe that we see
conflicting pictures of the mountain lion through
the eyes of hunters, ranchers, scientists,
wildlife managers, and preservationists. Each
viewpoint, like a piece of glass in a
kaleidoscope, is a shard, a fragment until it is
combined with the other pieces to create a total
image (137).

BORROWED LANGUAGE IN QUOTATION MARKS

McCall and Dutcher observe that "hunters,
ranchers, scientists, wildlife managers, and
preservationists" see the mountain lion quite
differently: "Each viewpoint, like a piece of
glass in a kaleidoscope, is a shard, a fragment
until it is combined with the other pieces to
create a total image" (137).

Putting summaries and paraphrases in your own words. When
you summarize or paraphrase, you must restate the
source's meaning using your own language. In the example at the top of page 112, the paraphrase is plagiarized—even though the source is cited—because too
much of its language is borrowed from the source. The
underlined strings of words have been copied word-for-
word (without quotation marks). In addition, the writer
has closely followed the sentence structure of the original source, merely plugging in some synonyms (*children* for *minors, brutally* for *severely,* and *assault* for *attack*).

ORIGINAL SOURCE

The park [Caspers Wilderness Park] was closed to
minors in 1992 after the family of a girl severely

mauled there in 1986 won a suit against the county.
The award of $2.1 million for the mountain lion
attack on Laura Small, who was 5 at the time, was
later reduced to $1.5 million.
　　　—Reyes and Messina, "More Warning Signs," p. B1

PLAGIARISM: UNACCEPTABLE BORROWING

Reyes and Messina report that Caspers Wilderness
Park was closed to children in 1992 after the
family of a girl brutally mauled there in 1986
sued the county. The family was ultimately
awarded $1.5 million for the mountain lion
assault on Laura Small, who was 5 at the time
(B1).

To avoid plagiarizing an author's language, set the
source aside, write from memory, and consult the source
later to check for accuracy. This strategy prevents you
from being captivated by the words on the page.

ACCEPTABLE PARAPHRASE

In 1992, officials banned minors from Caspers
Wilderness Park. Reyes and Messina explain that
park officials took this measure after a mountain
lion attack on a child led to a lawsuit. The
child, five-year-old Laura Small, had been
severely mauled by a lion in 1986, and her
parents sued the county. Eventually they received
an award of $1.5 million (B1).

29 Integrating nonfiction sources

When using the Modern Language Association's in-text
citations, use present tense or present perfect tense
verbs in phrases that introduce quotations or other
source material from nonfiction sources: *Perry points out
that* or *Perry has pointed out that* (not *Perry pointed out
that*). If you have good reason to emphasize that the author's language or opinion was articulated in the past,
however, the past tense is acceptable.

29a. Integrating quotations

Readers need to move from your own words to the words of a source without feeling a jolt.

Using signal phrases.   Avoid dropping quotations into the text without warning. Instead, provide clear signal phrases, usually including the author's name, to prepare readers for a quotation.

DROPPED QUOTATION

California law prevents the killing of mountain lions except for specific lions that have been proved to be a threat to humans or livestock. "Fish and Game is even blocked from keeping mountain lions from killing the endangered desert bighorn sheep" (Perry B4).

QUOTATION WITH SIGNAL PHRASE

California law prevents the killing of mountain lions except for specific lions that have been proved to be a threat to humans or livestock. Tony Perry points out that, ironically, "Fish and Game is even blocked from keeping mountain lions from killing the endangered desert bighorn sheep" (B4).

To avoid monotony, try to vary both the language and the placement of your signal phrases.

In the words of lion researcher Maurice Hornocker, " . . . "

As Kevin Hansen has noted, " . . . "

Karen McCall and Jim Dutcher point out that " . . . "

" . . . ," claims CLAW spokesperson Stephani Cruickshank.

" . . . ," writes Rychnovsky, " . . . "

California politician Tim Leslie offers an odd argument for this view:

Jerome Robinson answers these objections with the following analysis:

When your signal phrase includes a verb, choose one that is appropriate in the context. Is your source arguing a point, making an observation, reporting a fact, drawing a conclusion, refuting an argument, or stating a belief? By choosing an appropriate verb, such as one on the following list, you can make your source's stance clear.

acknowledges	comments	endorses	reasons
adds	compares	grants	refutes
admits	confirms	illustrates	rejects
agrees	contends	implies	reports
argues	declares	insists	responds
asserts	denies	notes	suggests
believes	disputes	observes	thinks
claims	emphasizes	points out	writes

Limiting your use of quotations. Except for the following legitimate uses of quotations, use your own words to summarize and paraphrase your sources and to explain your own ideas.

WHEN TO USE QUOTATIONS

— When language is especially vivid or expressive

— When exact wording is needed for technical accuracy

— When it is important to let the debaters of an issue explain their positions in their own words

— When the words of an important authority lend weight to an argument

— When the language of a source is the topic of your discussion (as in an analysis or interpretation)

It is not always necessary to quote full sentences from a source. To reduce your reliance on the words of others, you can often integrate a phrase from a source into your own sentence structure.

```
Uncommon as lion sightings may be, they are
highly publicized. As George Laycock points out,
a lion sighting in southern California "can push
Pope, President, or the Los Angeles Dodgers off
the front page" (88).
```

Jeff Rennike notes that Montana recorded no confirmed attacks by lions on humans "in its entire history prior to 1989" but has since tallied "as many as twenty-five incidents in a single year" (30).

Using the ellipsis mark.   To condense a quoted passage, you can use the ellipsis mark (three periods, with spaces between) to indicate that you have omitted words. What remains must be grammatically complete. MLA now recommends putting brackets around ellipsis dots (to indicate that the dots do not appear in the source).

The title of John Seidensticker's article poses a question: "Mountain lions don't stalk people. True or False?" The answer, writes Seidensticker, is "False. In the old West, the big cats were nearly wiped out, but [...] they are back--and going on the attack" (113).

On the rare occasions when you want to omit a full sentence or more, use a period before the three ellipsis dots.

Michael Milstein, a former ranger for the National Park Service, reports that the eastern cougar "is probably already extinct. [...] Though rare reports of sightings still surface, a recent search by the U.S. Fish and Wildlife Service failed to turn up any sightings" (20).

Ordinarily, do not use an ellipsis mark at the beginning or at the end of a quotation. Your readers will understand that the quoted material is taken from a longer passage, so such marks are not necessary. The only exception occurs when words at the end of the final quoted sentence have been dropped. In such cases, put bracketed ellipsis dots before the closing quotation mark and parenthetical reference: [. . .]" (103).

Obviously you should not use an ellipsis mark to distort the meaning of your source.

Using brackets.   Brackets (square parentheses) allow you to insert words of your own into quoted material. You can insert words in brackets to clarify matters or to keep a sentence grammatical in your context.

According to Tony Perry of the Los Angeles Times, "The mountain lion [in California] has never been in danger of extinction, not even during the 56 years (1907-1963) when several rural counties in California tried to eradicate lions by paying bounties to hunters" (B4).

The writer has added "in California" in brackets to make the context of Perry's claim clear: Perry is writing about California lions, not about lions in states (such as Florida) where the lion has faced extinction.

To indicate an error in a quotation, insert [sic] right after the error or (sic) after the closing quotation mark. Notice that the term "sic" is neither underlined nor italicized in MLA style.

According to Smith, Kistler's performance was brilliant, "exceding [sic] the expectations of even her most loyal fans" (B1).

Setting off long quotations.   When you quote more than four typed lines of prose, set off the quotation by indenting it one inch (or ten spaces) from the left margin. Use the normal right margin and do not single-space.

Long quotations should be introduced by an informative sentence, usually followed by a colon. Quotation marks are unnecessary because the indented format tells readers that the words are taken directly from the source.

Lion researcher Maurice Hornocker offers some practical advice to hikers:

> Visitors to lion habitat should carry a big stick and make noise as they hike to let the animal know they are approaching. Lions are intimidated by height, so if a cougar is sighted in the area, parents should put their children on their shoulders. If attacked, a person should not run, nor

```
should he play dead. Stand firm, fight
back, and yell--most people who have
resisted attack have successfully fought
off the lion. (60)
```

Notice that at the end of an indented quotation the parenthetical citation goes outside the final period. (When a quotation runs into your text, the opposite is true. See the sample citation at the top of p. 116.)

29b. Integrating summaries and paraphrases

Introduce most summaries and paraphrases with a signal phrase that names the author and places the material in context. Readers will then understand that everything between the signal phrase and the parenthetical citation summarizes or paraphrases the cited source.

Without the signal phrase (underlined) in the following example, readers might think that only the last sentence is being cited, when in fact most of the paragraph is based on the source.

```
    For much of this century, the U.S. government
has encouraged the extermination of mountain lions
and other wild animals. Sketching a brief history,
Kevin Hansen tells us that in 1915 Congress appro-
priated funds to wipe out animals that were
attacking cattle, and the U.S. Biological Survey
hired hunters and trappers to accomplish the
mission. Then, in 1931, the government stepped up
its efforts with the passage of the Animal Damage
Control Act, nicknamed "All Dead Critters" by its
critics. Between 1937 and 1970, reports Hansen,
over seven thousand mountain lions were killed by
Animal Damage Control (57).
```

29c. Integrating statistics and other facts

When you are citing a statistic or other specific fact, a signal phrase is often not necessary. In most cases, readers will understand that the citation refers to the statistic or fact (not the whole paragraph).

```
Even road kill statistics confirm the dramatic
increase in California lions. In the 1970s only
```

```
one or two lions were killed on state highways,
but twenty-five to thirty were killed in 1989
alone (Turback 74).
```

There is nothing wrong, however, with using a signal phrase to introduce a statistic or other fact.

```
Gary Turback observes that even road kill
statistics confirm the dramatic increase in
California lions. In the 1970s, he says, only one
or two lions were killed on California highways,
but twenty-five to thirty were killed in 1989
alone (74).
```

30 | Integrating literary quotations

Integrating quotations from a literary work smoothly into your own text can present a challenge. Because of the complexities of literature, do not be surprised to find yourself puzzling over the most graceful way to tuck in a short phrase or the clearest way to introduce a more extended passage from the work.

NOTE: The parenthetical citations at the ends of examples in this section tell readers where the quoted words can be found. They indicate the lines of a poem; the act, scene, and lines of a play; or the page number of a quotation from a short story or novel. (For guidelines on citing literary works, see pp. 124–25.)

30a. Introducing literary quotations

When writing about nonfiction essays and books, you have probably learned to introduce a quotation with a signal phrase naming the author: *According to Jane Doe, Jane Doe points out that, Jane Doe presents a compelling argument,* and so on.

When introducing quotations from a literary work, however, make sure that you don't confuse the work's author with the narrator of a story, the speaker of a poem, or a character in a play. Instead of naming the author, you can refer to the narrator or speaker—or to the work itself.

INAPPROPRIATE

Poet Andrew Marvell describes his fear of death like this: "But at my back I always hear / Time's wingèd chariot hurrying near" (21–22).

APPROPRIATE

Addressing his beloved in an attempt to win her sexual favors, the speaker of the poem argues that death gives them no time to waste: "But at my back I always hear / Time's wingèd chariot hurrying near" (21–22).

APPROPRIATE

The poem "To His Coy Mistress" says as much about fleeting time and death as it does about sexual passion. Its most powerful lines may well be "But at my back I always hear / Time's wingèd chariot hurrying near" (21–22).

In the last example, you could of course mention the author as well: *Marvell's poem "To His Coy Mistress" says as much. . . .* Although the author is mentioned, he is not being confused with the speaker of the poem.

If you are quoting the words of a character in a story or a play, you should name the character who is speaking and provide a context for the spoken words. In the following examples, the quoted dialogue is from Tennessee Williams's play *The Glass Menagerie* and Shirley Jackson's short story "The Lottery."

Laura's life is so completely ruled by Amanda that when urged to make a wish on the moon, she asks, "What shall I wish for, Mother?" (1.5.140).

When a neighbor suggests that the lottery be abandoned, Old Man Warner responds, "There's *always* been a lottery" (284).

30b. Avoiding shifts in tense

Because it is conventional to write about literature in the present tense (see pp. 9–10) and because literary works often use other tenses, you will need to exercise some care when weaving quotations into your own text. A first-draft attempt may result in an awkward shift, as it did for one student who was writing about Nadine Gordimer's short story "Friday's Footprint."

TENSE SHIFT

> When Rita sees Johnny's relaxed attitude, "she blushed, like a wave of illness" (159).

To avoid the distracting shift from present to past tense, the writer decided to include the reference to Rita's blushing in her own text and reduce the length of the quotation.

REVISED

> When Rita sees Johnny's relaxed attitude, she blushes, "like a wave of illness" (159).

The writer could have changed the quotation to present tense, using brackets to indicate the change, like this: *When Rita sees Johnny's relaxed attitude, "she blushe[s], like a wave of illness" (159).* However, using brackets around just one letter of a word can seem pedantic, so the earlier revision is preferable. (For advice on using brackets around a word or more, see pp. 115–16.)

30c. Formatting literary quotations

Guidelines for formatting quotations from short stories (or novels), poems, and plays are slightly different from one another.

Short stories or novels. If a quotation from a short story or a novel takes up four or fewer typed lines, put it in quotation marks and run it into the text of your essay. Include a page number in parentheses after the quotation.

> The narrator of Eudora Welty's "Why I Live at the PO," known to us only as "Sister," makes many catty remarks about her enemies. For example, she calls Mr. Whitaker "this photographer with the pop-eyes" (46).

If a quotation from a short story or a novel is five typed lines or longer, set it off from the text by indenting one inch (or ten spaces) from the left margin; when you set a quotation off from the text, you should not use quotation marks around it. (See also pp. 116–17.) Put the page number in parentheses after the final mark of punctuation.

Sister's tale begins with "I," and she makes every
event revolve around herself, even her sister's
marriage:

> I was getting along fine with Mama, Papa-
> Daddy, and Uncle Rondo until my sister
> Stella-Rondo just separated from her
> husband and came back home again. Mr.
> Whitaker! Of course I went with Mr.
> Whitaker first, when he first appeared here
> in China Grove, taking "Pose Yourself" pho-
> tos, and Stella-Rondo broke us up. (46)

Poems. Enclose quotations of three or fewer lines of
poetry in quotation marks within your text, and indicate
line breaks with a slash. Include line numbers in parentheses at the end of the quotation.

> The opening lines of Frost's "Fire and Ice" strike a
> conversational tone: "Some say the world will end in
> fire, / Some say in ice" (1–2).

When you quote four or more lines of poetry, set
the quotation off from the text by indenting one inch
(or ten spaces) and omit the quotation marks. Put the
line numbers in parentheses after the final mark of
punctuation.

> The opening stanza of Louise Bogan's "Women" star-
> tles readers by presenting a negative stereotype of
> women:
>
> > Women have no wilderness in them,
> > They are provident instead,
> > Content in the tight hot cell of their hearts
> > To eat dusty bread. (1–4)

Plays. If a quotation from a character in a play takes
up four or fewer typed lines, put quotation marks around
it and run it into the text of your essay. Whenever possible, include the act number, scene number, and line
numbers in parentheses at the end of the quotation.
Separate the numbers with periods, and use arabic numerals unless your instructor prefers roman numerals.

> Two attendants silently watch as the sleepwalking
> Lady Macbeth subconsciously struggles with her
> guilt: "Here's the smell of blood still. All the perfumes
> of Arabia will not sweeten this little hand" (5.1.50–51).

If a quotation from a character in a play is five lines or longer, set it off in the same way you would set off a long prose quotation. Include the act number, scene number, and line numbers after the final mark of punctuation.

31 MLA documentation style

To document sources, the Modern Language Association (MLA) recommends in-text citations that refer readers to a list of works cited. (For recent updates in MLA's system for documenting Internet sources, go to the following Web site: <http://www.mla.org/set_stl.htm>)

31a. MLA in-text citations

MLA in-text citations are made with a combination of signal phrases and parenthetical references. Usually the signal phrase mentions the author's name; the parenthetical reference includes at least a page number (unless the work has no page numbers or is organized alphabetically).

1. AUTHOR NAMED IN A SIGNAL PHRASE. Naming the author in a signal phrase allows you to keep the parenthetical citation brief. Usually only a page number is required.

```
Turback claims that "regulated sport hunting has
never driven any wild species into extinction"
(74).
```

The signal phrase—"Turback claims that"—provides the name of the author; the parenthetical citation gives the page number where the quoted words may be found. By looking up the author's last name in the list of works cited, readers will find complete information about the work's title, publisher, and place and date of publication.

2. AUTHOR NOT NAMED IN A SIGNAL PHRASE. If the signal phrase does not include the author's name (or if there is no signal phrase), the author's last name must appear in parentheses along with the page number.

```
Though the number of lion attacks on humans is
low, the rate of increase of attacks since the
1960s is cause for serious concern (Rychnovsky
43).
```

3. TWO OR MORE WORKS BY THE SAME AUTHOR. If your list of works cited includes two or more works by the same author, include the title of the work in the signal phrase or use a short form of the title in the parenthetical reference.

```
In his article "California and the West,"
reporter T. Christian Miller asserts that from
1990 to 1997, California spent roughly $26
million on conservation lands "to provide habitat
for exactly 2.6 mountain lions" (A3).
```

```
According to T. Christian Miller, "Mountain lions,
also called pumas or cougars, range vast terri-
tories in search of food, sometimes as large as
100 square miles" ("Cougars" 1).
```

4. TWO OR THREE AUTHORS. Name all the authors in the signal phrase or include them in the parenthetical reference.

Reyes and Messina report that the adult mountain lion population in California is now estimated at four to six thousand (B1).

5. FOUR OR MORE AUTHORS. Include only the first author's name followed by "et al." (Latin for "and others") in the signal phrase or in the parenthetical reference.

The study was extended for two years, and only after results were duplicated on both coasts did the authors publish their results (Doe et al. 137).

6. CORPORATE AUTHOR. Name the corporate author in the signal phrase or include a shortened version in the parentheses.

The Internal Revenue Service warns businesses that deductions for "lavish and extravagant entertainment" are not allowed (43).

7. UNKNOWN AUTHOR. If the author is not given, either use the complete title in a signal phrase or use a short form of the title in the parentheses.

In California, fish and game officials estimate that since 1972 lion numbers have increased from 2,400 to at least 6,000 ("Lion" A21).

8. AUTHORS WITH THE SAME LAST NAME. Include the first name of the author you are citing in the signal phrase or parenthetical reference.

At least 66,665 lions were killed between 1907 and 1978 in Canada and the United States (Kevin Hansen 58).

9. A MULTIVOLUME WORK. If your paper cites more than one volume of a multivolume work, indicate in the parentheses the volume you are referring to, followed by a colon.

Terman's studies of gifted children reveal a pattern of accelerated language acquisition (2: 279).

10. A NOVEL, A PLAY, OR A POEM. Include information that will enable readers to find the passage in various editions of the work. For a novel, put the page number first and then, if possible, indicate the part or chapter in which the passage can be found.

One of Kingsolver's narrators, teenager Rachel, pushes her vocabulary beyond its limits. For example, Rachel complains that being forced to live in the Congo with her missionary family is "a sheer tapestry of justice" because her chances of finding a boyfriend are "dull and void" (177; bk. 2, ch. 10).

For a verse play, list the act, scene, and line numbers, separated by periods. Use arabic numerals.

In his famous advice to the players, Shakespeare's Hamlet defines the purpose of theater, "whose end, both at the first and now, was and is, to hold, as 'twere, the mirror up to nature" (3.2.21-23).

For a poem, cite the part (if there are a number of parts) and the line numbers, separated by periods.

When Homer's Odysseus comes to the hall of Circe, he finds his men "mild / in her soft spell, fed on her drug of evil" (10.209-11).

11. THE BIBLE. Include the version of the Bible, the book of the Bible, and the chapter and verse numbers either in the signal phrase or in the parentheses.

Consider the words of Solomon: "If your enemies are hungry, give them bread to eat; and if they are thirsty, give them water to drink" (New Revised Standard Bible, Prov. 25.21).

12. A WORK IN AN ANTHOLOGY. Put the name of the author of the work (not the editor of the anthology) in the signal phrase or in the parentheses.

At the end of Kate Chopin's "The Story of an Hour," Mrs. Mallard drops dead upon learning that her husband is alive. In the final irony of the story, doctors report that she has died of a "joy that kills" (25).

13. AN ENTIRE WORK. To cite an entire work, use the author's name in a signal phrase or a parenthetical reference.

```
Robinson succinctly describes the status of the
mountain lion controversy in California.
```

14. TWO OR MORE WORKS To cite more than one source to document a particular point, separate the citations with a semicolon.

```
The dangers of mountain lions to humans have been
well documented (Rychnovsky 40; Seidensticker 114;
Williams 30).
```

15. A WORK WITHOUT PAGE NUMBERS. You may omit the page number if a work has no page numbers or if a work is only one page long or is organized alphabetically (as with encyclopedias). Some electronic sources use paragraph numbers instead of page numbers. For such sources, use the abbreviation "par." or "pars." in the parentheses: (Smith, par. 4).

16. AN ELECTRONIC SOURCE. To cite an electronic source in the text of your paper, follow the same rules as for print sources. If the source has an author and there is a page number, provide both.

```
Using historical writings about leprosy as an
example, Demaitre argues that "the difference
between curability and treatability is not a
modern invention" (29).
```

Electronic sources often lack page numbers. If the source uses some other numbering system, such as paragraphs or sections, specify them, using an abbreviation ("par.," "sec.") or a full word ("screen"). Otherwise, use no number at all.

If the electronic source has no known author, either use the complete title in a signal phrase or use a short form of the title in parentheses.

```
According to a Web page sponsored by the
Children's Defense Fund, fourteen American
children die from gunfire each day ("Child").
```

17. AN INDIRECT SOURCE. When a writer's or speaker's quoted words appear in a source written by someone else, begin the citation with the abbreviation "qtd. in."

"When lion sightings become common," says Fjelline, trouble often follows" (qtd. in Robinson 30).

31b. MLA list of works cited

An alphabetized list of works cited, which appears at the end of your paper, gives full publication information for each of the sources you have cited in the paper. For advice on constructing the list and typing it according to MLA guidelines, see section 32. A sample list of works cited appears on page 141.

The following models illustrate the MLA form for entries in the list of works cited.

Books

1. BASIC FORMAT FOR A BOOK. For most books, arrange the information into three units, each followed by a period and one space: (1) the author's name, last name first; (2) the title and subtitle, underlined or italicized; and (3) the place of publication, the publisher, and the date.

Tannen, Deborah. The Argument Culture: Moving from
    Debate to Dialogue. New York: Random, 1998.

2. TWO OR THREE AUTHORS

Rosenfeld, Louis, Joseph Janes, and Martha Vander
    Holk. The Internet Compendium: Subject Guides
    to Humanities Resources. New York: Neal,
    1995.

3. FOUR OR MORE AUTHORS

Holloway, Susan D., et al. Through My Own Eyes:
    Single Mothers and the Cultures of Poverty.
    Cambridge: Harvard UP, 1997.

4. EDITORS

Kitchen, Judith, and Mary Paumier Jones, eds. In
    Short: A Collection of Brief Creative
    Nonfiction. New York: Norton, 1996.

5. AUTHOR WITH AN EDITOR

Wells, Ida B. The Memphis Diary. Ed. Miriam
    DeCosta-Willis. Boston: Beacon, 1995.

6. TRANSLATION

Mahfouz, Naguib. Arabian Nights and Days. Trans.
    Denys Johnson-Davies. New York: Doubleday,
    1995.

7. CORPORATE AUTHOR

Bank of Boston. Bank by Remote Control. Boston:
    Bank of Boston, 1997.

8. UNKNOWN AUTHOR

Oxford Essential World Atlas. New York: Oxford
    UP, 1996.

9. TWO OR MORE WORKS BY THE SAME AUTHOR

Updike, John. In The Beauty of the Lilies. New
    York: Knopf, 1996.

———. Toward the End of Time. New York: Knopf,
    1997.

10. EDITION OTHER THAN THE FIRST

Boyce, David George. The Irish Question and
    British Politics, 1868-1996. 2nd ed. New
    York: St. Martin's, 1996.

11. MULTIVOLUME WORK

Conway, Jill Ker, ed. Written by Herself. 2 vols.
    New York: Random, 1996.

12. ENCYCLOPEDIA OR DICTIONARY

"Sonata." Encyclopaedia Britannica. 15th ed. 1997.

13. THE BIBLE

New American Bible. New York: Catholic Book
    Publishing, 1970.

14. WORK IN AN ANTHOLOGY

Malouf, David. "The Kyogle Line." The Oxford Book
    of Travel Stories. Ed. Patricia Craig.
    Oxford: Oxford UP, 1996. 390-96.

15. TWO OR MORE WORKS FROM THE SAME ANTHOLOGY

Craig, Patricia, ed. The Oxford Book of Travel
    Stories. Oxford: Oxford UP, 1996.

Desai, Anita. "Scholar and Gypsy." Craig 251-73.

Malouf, David. "The Kyogle Line." Craig 390-96.

16. FOREWORD, INTRODUCTION, PREFACE, OR AFTERWORD

Kennedy, Edward M. Foreword. Make a Difference.
    By Henry W. Foster, Jr., and Alice Greenwood.
    New York: Scribner, 1997. 9-15.

17. BOOK WITH A TITLE WITHIN ITS TITLE

Vanderham, Paul. James Joyce and Censorship: The
        Trials of Ulysses. New York: New York UP, 1997.

18. BOOK IN A SERIES

Malena, Anne. The Dynamics of Identity in
        Francophone Caribbean Narrative. Francophone
        Cultures and Literatures Ser. 24. New York:
        Lang, 1998.

19. REPUBLISHED BOOK

McClintock, Walter. Old Indian Trails. 1926.
        Foreword William Least Heat Moon. Boston:
        Houghton, 1992.

20. PUBLISHER'S IMPRINT

Coles, Robert. The Moral Intelligence of Children:
        How to Raise a Moral Child. New York: Plume-
        Random, 1997.

Articles in periodicals

NOTE: When an article's pages are not consecutive, give
the number of the first page followed by a plus sign: 32+.

21. ARTICLE IN A MONTHLY MAGAZINE

Kaplan, Robert D. "History Moving North." Atlantic
        Monthly Feb. 1997: 21+.

22. ARTICLE IN A WEEKLY MAGAZINE

Pierpont, Claudia Roth. "A Society of One: Zora
        Neale Hurston, American Contrarian." New
        Yorker 17 Feb. 1997: 80-86.

23. ARTICLE IN A JOURNAL PAGINATED BY VOLUME

Cheuse, Alan. "Narrative Painting and Pictorial
        Fiction." Antioch Review 55 (1997): 277-91.

24. ARTICLE IN A JOURNAL PAGINATED BY ISSUE

Dennis, Carl. "What Is Our Poetry to Make of Ancient
        Myths?" New England Review 18.4 (1997): 128-40.

25. ARTICLE IN A DAILY NEWSPAPER

Knox, Richard A. "Please Don't Dial and Drive,
    Study Suggests." Boston Globe 13 Feb. 1997:
    A1+.

26. UNSIGNED ARTICLE IN A NEWSPAPER OR MAGAZINE

"Marines Charged in Assault Case." Houston
    Chronicle 14 Feb. 1998: 6A.

27. EDITORIAL IN A NEWSPAPER

"Health Risk on Tap." Editorial. Los Angeles
    Times 11 Feb. 1998: B6.

28. LETTER TO THE EDITOR

Peters, Tom. Letter. New Yorker 16 Feb. 1998: 13.

29. BOOK OR FILM REVIEW

France, Peter. "His Own Biggest Hero." Rev. of
    Victor Hugo, by Graham Robb. New York Times
    Book Review 15 Jan. 1998: 7.

Taubin, Amy. "Year of the Lady." Rev. of The
    Portrait of a Lady, dir. Jane Campion.
    Village Voice 7 Jan. 1997: 64.

Electronic sources

The documentation style for electronic sources presented in this section is consistent with MLA's most recent guidelines, which can be found at <http://
www.mla.org/set_stl.htm> or in the *MLA Handbook for
Writers of Research Papers* (5th ed., 1999).

NOTE: When an Internet address in a works cited entry
must be divided at the end of a line, break it after a
slash. Do not insert a hyphen.

30. ONLINE SCHOLARLY PROJECT OR REFERENCE DATABASE

Dickinson, Emily. "Hope." Poems by Emily
    Dickinson. 3rd ser. Boston, 1896. Project
    Bartleby Archive. Ed. Steven van Leeuwen. 15
    Dec. 1995. Columbia U. 11 June 1999

<http://www.columbia.edu/acis/bartleby/
dickinson/dickinson1.html#3>.

"Gog and Magog." The Encyclopedia Mythica. Ed.
Micha F. Lindemans. 24 May 1999. 10 June
1999 <http://www.pantheon.org/mythica/
articles/g/gog_and_magog.html>.

31. PERSONAL OR PROFESSIONAL WEB SITE

Spanoudis, Steve, Bob Blair, and Nelson Miller.
Poets' Corner. 7 June 1999. 13 June 1999
<http://www.geocities.com/~spanoudi/poems>.

Blue Note Records. 9 June 1999. Blue Note
Records. 9 June 1999 <http://
www.bluenote.com>.

32. ONLINE BOOK

Shelley, Mary. Frankenstein. An Online Library of
Literature. Ed. Peter Galbavy. 14 Feb. 1999.
23 June 1999 <http://www.literature.org/
Works/Mary-Shelley/frankenstein>.

33. ARTICLE IN AN ONLINE PERIODICAL

Coontz, Stephanie. "Family Myths, Family
Realities." Salon 12 Dec. 1997. 3 Feb. 2000
<http://www.salonmagazine.com/mwt/feature/
1997/12/23coontz.html>.

34. WORK FROM AN ONLINE SUBSCRIPTION SERVICE

Sleek, Scott. "Blame Your Peers, Not Your
Parents, Author Says." APA Monitor 29.1
(1998). America Online. 1 Mar. 1999. Keyword:
The Nurture Assumption.

Miller, Christian. "Cougars Reported in Tarzana,
Woodland Hills." Los Angeles Times 25 Nov.
1997: Metro 1. Electric Lib. O'Neill Lib.,
Boston College, Chestnut Hill, MA. 12 Mar.
1998 <http://www.elibrary.com>.

35. ONLINE POSTING

Crosby, Connie. "Literary Criticism." Online
    posting. 2 Feb. 1996. Café Utne. 17 Mar.
    1998 <http://www.utne.com/motet/bin/
    show?-u4Lsul+it-la+Literature+12>.

36. E-MAIL

Schubert, Josephine. "Re: Culture Shock." E-mail
    to the author. 14 Mar. 2000.

37. SYNCHRONOUS COMMUNICATION

Kelley, Heather. Jill's Borderland Tour of DU. 14
    Dec. 1995. Borderlands MOOspace. 16 Mar. 1998
    <http://www.cyberstation.net/~idd/v2/
    bordj24.htm>.

38. OTHER ONLINE SOURCES

"No More Kings." Animation. America Rock.
    Schoolhouse Rock. ABC. 1975. 16 Mar. 2000
    <http://genxtvland.simplenet.com/
    SchoolHouseRock/song.hts?hi+kings>.

"City of New Orleans, LA." Map. Yahoo! Maps.
    Yahoo! 1998. 4 Feb. 1998 <http://
    maps.yahoo.com/yahoo>.

39. CD-ROM ISSUED IN A SINGLE EDITION

Sheehy, Donald, ed. Robert Frost: Poems, Life,
    Legacy. CD-ROM. New York: Holt, 1997.

"Picasso, Pablo." The 1997 Grolier Multimedia
    Encyclopedia. CD-ROM. Danbury: Grolier, 1997.

40. CD-ROM ISSUED PERIODICALLY

Bohlen, Celestine. "Albania Struggles to Contain
    Dissent over Lost Investments." New York
    Times 11 Feb. 1997, late ed.: A9. InfoTrac:
    General Periodicals ASAP. CD-ROM. Information
    Access. 13 Feb. 1997.

Wattenberg, Ruth. "Helping Students in the
    Middle." American Educator 19.4 (1996): 2-18.
    ERIC. CD-ROM. SilverPlatter. Sept. 1996.

Other sources

41. GOVERNMENT PUBLICATION

United States. Bureau of the Census. Statistical
Abstract of the United States. 117th ed.
Washington: GPO, 1997.

42. PAMPHLET

United States. Dept. of the Interior. Natl. Park
Service. National Design Competition for an
Indian Memorial: Little Bighorn Battlefield
National Monument. Washington, GPO, 1996.

43. PUBLISHED DISSERTATION

Damberg, Cheryl L. Healthcare Reform:
Distributional Consequences of an Employer
Mandate for Workers in Small Firms. Diss.
Rand Graduate School, 1995. Santa Monica:
Rand, 1996.

44. UNPUBLISHED DISSERTATION

Healey, Catherine. "Joseph Conrad's
Impressionism." Diss. U of Massachusetts,
1997.

45. DISSERTATION ABSTRACT

Chun, Maria Bow Jun. "A Study of Multicultural
Activities in Hawaii's Public Schools." Diss.
U of Hawaii, 1996. DAI 57 (1997): 2813A.

46. PUBLISHED PROCEEDINGS OF A CONFERENCE

Chattel, Servant, or Citizen: Women's Status in
Church, State, and Society. Proc. of Irish
Conf. of Historians, 1993, Belfast. Belfast:
Inst. of Irish Studies, 1995.

47. WORK OF ART

Constable, John. Dedham Vale. Victoria and Albert
Museum, London.

48. MUSICAL COMPOSITION

Copland, Aaron. Appalachian Spring.

Shostakovich, Dmitri. Quartet no. 1 in C, op. 49.

49. PERSONAL LETTER

Cipriani, Karen. Letter to the author. 25 Apr.
1998.

50. LECTURE OR PUBLIC ADDRESS

Middleton, Frank. "Louis Hayden and the Role of
the Underground Railroad in Boston." Boston
Public Lib., Boston. 6 Feb. 1998.

51. PERSONAL INTERVIEW

Meeker, Dolores. Personal interview. 21 Apr. 1998.

52. PUBLISHED INTERVIEW

Renoir, Jean. "Renoir at Home: Interview with Jean
Renoir." Film Quarterly 50.1 (1996): 2-8.

53. RADIO OR TELEVISION INTERVIEW

Gates, Henry Louis, Jr. Interview. Charlie Rose.
PBS. WNET, New York. 13 Feb. 1997.

54. FILM OR VIDEOTAPE

The English Patient. Dir. Anthony Minghella. Perf.
Ralph Fiennes, Juliette Binoche, Willem Dafoe,
and Kristin Scott Thomas. Miramax, 1996.

Jane Eyre. Dir. Robert Young. Perf. Samantha
Morton and Ciaran Hinds. Videocassette. New
Video Group, 1997.

55. RADIO OR TELEVISION PROGRAM

"The New Face of Africa." The Connection. Host
Christopher Lydon. Natl. Public Radio. WBUR,
Boston. 27 Mar. 1998.

Primates. Wild Discovery. Discovery Channel. 23
Mar. 1998.

56. LIVE PERFORMANCE OF A PLAY

Six Characters in Search of an Author. By Luigi
Pirandello. Dir. Robert Brustein. Perf.
Jeremy Geidt, David Ackroyd, Monica Koskey,

and Marianne Owen. American Repertory

Theatre, Cambridge. 14 Jan. 1997.

57. SOUND RECORDING

Bizet, Georges. Carmen. Perf. Jennifer Larmore,

Thomas Moser, Angela Gheorghiu, and Samuel

Ramey. Bavarian State Orch. and Chorus. Cond.

Giuseppe Sinopoli. Warner, 1996.

58. CARTOON

Adams, Scott. "Dilbert." Cartoon. Editorial Humor

3 Mar. 1998: 9.

59. MAP OR CHART

Winery Guide to Northern and Central California.

Map. Modesto: Compass Maps, 1996.

31c. MLA information notes

Researchers who use the MLA system of parenthetical documentation may also use information notes for one of two purposes:

1. to provide additional material that might interrupt the flow of the paper yet is important enough to include;
2. to refer readers to any sources not discussed in the paper.

Information notes may be either footnotes or endnotes. Footnotes appear at the foot of the page; endnotes appear on a separate page at the end of the paper, just before the list of works cited. For either style, the notes are numbered consecutively throughout the paper. The text of the paper contains a raised arabic numeral that corresponds to the number of the note.

TEXT

California is not alone in its concern about

mountain lion attacks.[1]

NOTE

[1]For a discussion of lion attacks in other

western states, see Turback 34.

32 MLA manuscript format

The Modern Language Association makes the following recommendations about manuscript format.

Title and identification. MLA does not require a title page. On the first page of your paper, place your name, your instructor's name, the course title, and the date on separate lines against the left margin. Then center your title. (See. p. 140 for a sample first page.)

Margins, spacing, and indentation. Leave margins of at least one inch but no more than an inch and a half on all sides of the page. Do not justify the right margin.

Double-space between lines and indent the first line of each paragraph one-half inch (or five spaces) from the left margin.

For a quotation longer than four typed lines of prose or three lines of verse, indent each line one inch (or ten spaces) from the left margin. Double-space between the body of the paper and the quotation, and double-space the lines of the quotation.

Pagination. Using arabic numerals, number all pages in the upper right corner, one-half inch below the top edge. Put your last name before each page number for clear identification in case pages are misplaced.

Punctuation and typing. Leave one space after words, commas, colons, and semicolons and between dots in ellipsis marks. MLA allows either one or two spaces after periods, question marks, and exclamation points. To form a dash, type two hyphens with no space between them; do not put a space on either side of the dash.

When an Internet address mentioned in the text of your paper must be divided at the end of a line, do not insert a hyphen (a hyphen could appear to be part of the address). For advice on dividing Internet addresses in your list of works cited, see page 132.

Headings. MLA neither encourages nor discourages use of headings and currently provides no guidelines for their use. If you would like to use headings in a long essay or research paper, check first with your instructor.

Although headings are not used as frequently in English and the humanities as in other disciplines, the trend seems to be changing.

Visuals.   MLA classifies visuals as tables and figures (figures include graphs, charts, maps, photographs, and drawings). Label each table with an arabic numeral (Table 1, Table 2, and so on) and provide a clear caption that identifies the subject; the label and caption should appear on separate lines above the table. For each figure, a label and a caption are usually placed below the figure, and they need not appear on separate lines. The word "Figure" may be abbreviated to "Fig."

Visuals should be placed in the text, as close as possible to the sentences that relate to them, unless your instructor prefers them in an appendix.

Preparing the works cited page.   On page 141 is a sample list of works cited. The list of works cited appears at the end of the paper.

To construct such a list, begin on a new page and title your list "Works Cited." Alphabetize the list by the last names of the authors (or editors); if a work has no author or editor, alphabetize by the first word of the title other than *A, An,* or *The.*

If two or more works by the same author appear in the list, use the author's name only for the first entry. For subsequent entries, use three hyphens followed by a period. List the titles in alphabetical order.

Do not indent the first line of each entry in the list, but indent any additional lines one-half inch (or five spaces). Double-space throughout.

NOTE: The sample works cited page shows you how to type the list. For information about the exact format of each entry in the list of works cited, consult the models in section 31b.

SAMPLE MLA PAGE

Garcia 1

John Garcia

Professor Hacker

English 101

7 April 1999

The Mountain Lion:

Once Endangered, Now a Danger

On April 23, 1994, as Barbara Schoener was jogging in the Sierra foothills of California, she was pounced on from behind by a mountain lion. After an apparent struggle with her attacker, Schoener was killed by bites to her neck and head (Rychnovsky 39). In 1996, because of Schoener's death and other highly publicized attacks, California politicians presented voters with Proposition 197, which contained provisions repealing much of a 1990 law enacted to protect the lions. The 1990 law outlawed sport hunting of mountain lions and even prevented the Department of Fish and Game from thinning the lion population.

Proposition 197 was rejected by a large margin, probably because the debate turned into a struggle between hunting and antihunting factions. When California politicians revisit the mountain lion question, they should frame the issue in a new way. A future proposition should retain the ban on sport hunting but allow the Department of Fish and Game to control the population. Wildlife management would reduce the number of lion attacks on humans and in the long run would also protect the lions.

The once-endangered mountain lion

To early Native Americans, mountain lions-- also known as cougars, pumas, and panthers--were objects of reverence. The European colonists, however, did not share the Native American view. They conducted what Ted Williams calls an "all- out war on the species" (29).

SAMPLE MLA LIST OF WORKS CITED

Works Cited

California Wildlife Protection Coalition.
     California Mountain Lion Page. 27 Mar. 1996.
     Sierra Club. 24 Mar. 1999 <http://
     www.sierraclub.org/chapters/ca/
     mountain-lion>.

Eagan, Terrence M., Wayne Long, and Steven
     Arroyo. "Rebuttal to Argument against
     Proposition 197." *1996 California Primary
     Election Server*. 1996. California Secretary
     of State. 24 Mar. 1999 <http://
     primary96.ss.ca.gov/e/ballot/197again2.html>.

Hansen, Kevin. *Cougar: The American Lion*.
     Flagstaff: Northland, 1992.

Hornocker, Maurice G. "Learning to Live with
     Lions." *National Geographic* July 1992:
     37-65.

"Lion Attacks Prompt State to Respond." *New York
     Times* 18 Oct. 1995, late ed.: A21.

Perry, Tony. "Big Cat Fight." *Los Angeles Times* 8
     Mar. 1996, home ed.: B1+.

"Proposition 197: Text of Proposed Law." *1996
     California Primary Election Server*. 1996.
     California Secretary of State. 24 Mar. 1999
     <http://primary96.ss.ca.gov/e/ballot/
     197txt.html>.

Rychnovsky, Ray. "Clawing into Controversy."
     Outdoor Life Jan. 1995: 38-42.

Seidensticker, John. "Mountain Lions Don't Stalk
     People: True or False?" *Audubon* Feb. 1992:
     113-22.

Williams, Ted. "The Lion's Silent Return." *Audubon*
     Nov. 1994: 28-35.

A
P
A

APA Papers

Most writing assignments in the social sciences are either reports of original research or reviews of the literature written about a particular research topic. Often an original research report contains a "review of the literature" section that places the writer's project in the context of previous research.

When writing a review of the literature or any other social science paper that draws on written sources, you face three main challenges: (1) supporting a thesis, (2) documenting sources and avoiding plagiarism, and (3) integrating quotations and other source material. Most social science instructors will ask you to document sources with the American Psychological Association (APA) system of in-text citations described in section 36.

33 Supporting a thesis

A thesis, which usually appears at the end of the introduction, is a one-sentence (or occasionally a two-sentence) statement of your central idea. In a review of the literature paper, this thesis analyzes the often competing conclusions drawn by a variety of researchers.

33a. Finding a thesis

You will be reading articles and other sources that address a central research question. Your thesis will express a reasonable answer to that question, given the current state of research in the field. Here, for example, is a research question and a thesis that answers it.

RESEARCH QUESTION

How and to what extent have the great apes—gorillas, chimpanzees, and orangutans—demonstrated
language abilities akin to those of humans?

POSSIBLE THESIS

Researchers agree that apes have acquired fairly
large vocabularies in American Sign Language and
in artificial languages, but they have drawn quite
different conclusions in addressing the following
questions: (1) How spontaneously have apes used
language? (2) How creatively have apes used
language? (3) To what extent can apes create
sentences? (4) What are some implications of
the ape language studies?

33b. Organizing your evidence

The American Psychological Association encourages the
use of headings to help readers follow the organization
of a paper. If you decide to use headings, you will not
need to write a formal outline. Just list the headings (and
perhaps subheadings) and you will have a blueprint for
your paper. The student who wrote about apes and language used the four questions in her thesis as headings
for her paper. The first page of the text of the student's
paper appears on page 166.

34 Citing sources; avoiding plagiarism

In researched writing, you will be drawing on the work
of other writers, and you must document their contributions by citing your sources. Sources are cited for two
reasons: to tell readers where your information comes
from and to give credit to the writers from whom you
have borrowed words and ideas. To borrow another
writer's language or ideas without proper acknowledgment is a form of dishonesty known as *plagiarism*.

34a. Citing sources

Citations are required when you quote from a source,
when you summarize or paraphrase a source, and when
you borrow facts and ideas from a source (except for

common knowledge). The American Psychological Association recommends an author-date style of citations. Here, very briefly, is how the author-date system often works. See 36 for a detailed discussion of variations.

1. The source is introduced by a signal phrase that includes the last names of the authors followed by the date of publication in parentheses.
2. The material being cited is followed by a page number in parentheses.
3. At the end of the paper, a list of references (arranged alphabetically according to the authors' last names) gives complete publication information about the source.

IN-TEXT CITATION

Noting that the apes' brains are similar to those of our human ancestors, Leakey and Lewin (1992) argued that in ape brains "the cognitive foundations on which human language could be built are already present" (p. 244).

ENTRY IN THE LIST OF REFERENCES

Leakey, R., & Lewin, R. (1992). *Origins reconsidered: In search of what makes us human.* New York: Doubleday.

NOTE: APA recommends using a hanging indent, as just illustrated, in the list of references (see also page 163).

34b. Avoiding plagiarism

Your research paper is a collaboration between you and your sources. To be fair and ethical, you must acknowledge your debt to the writers of these sources. If you don't, you are guilty of plagiarism, a serious academic offense.

Three different acts are considered plagiarism: (1) failing to cite quotations and borrowed ideas, (2) failing to enclose borrowed language in quotation marks, and (3) failing to put summaries and paraphrases in your own words.

Citing quotations and borrowed ideas. You must of course document all direct quotations. You must also cite any ideas borrowed from a source: paraphrases of sentences, summaries of paragraphs or chapters, statistics and little-known facts, and tables, graphs, or diagrams.

The only exception is common knowledge — information that your readers could find in any number of general sources because it is commonly known. For example, the current population of the United States is common knowledge in such fields as sociology and economics; Freud's theory of the unconscious is common knowledge in the field of psychology.

As a rule, when you have seen certain information repeatedly in your reading, you don't need to cite it. However, when information has appeared in only one or two sources or when it is controversial, you should cite it. If a topic is new to you and you are not sure what is considered common knowledge or what is controversial, ask someone with expertise. When in doubt, cite the source.

Enclosing borrowed language in quotation marks. To indicate that you are using a source's exact phrases or sentences, you must enclose them in quotation marks unless they have been set off from the text by indenting. (See 35a.) To omit the quotation marks is to claim — falsely — that the language is your own. Such an omission is plagiarism even if you have cited the source.

ORIGINAL SOURCE

No animal has done more to renew interest in animal intelligence than a beguiling, bilingual bonobo named Kanzi, who has the grammatical abilities of a 2½-year-old child and a taste for movies about cavemen.

—Linden, "Animals," p. 57

PLAGIARISM

```
According to Linden (1986), no animal has done
more to renew interest in animal intelligence
than a beguiling, bilingual bonobo named Kanzi,
who has the grammatical abilities of a 2-1/2-
year-old child and a taste for movies about
cavemen (p. 57).
```

BORROWED LANGUAGE IN QUOTATION MARKS

According to Linden (1986), "No animal has done more to renew interest in animal intelligence than a beguiling, bilingual bonobo named Kanzi, who has the grammatical abilities of a 2-1/2-year-old child and a taste for movies about cavemen" (p. 57).

Putting summaries and paraphrases in your own words. When you summarize or paraphrase, you must restate the source's meaning using your own language. You are guilty of plagiarism if you half-copy the author's sentences — either by mixing the author's well-chosen phrases without using quotation marks or by plugging your own synonyms into the author's sentence structure. The following paraphrases are plagiarized — even though the source is cited — because their language is too close to that of the source.

ORIGINAL SOURCE

If the existence of a signing ape was unsettling for linguists, it was also startling news for animal behaviorists. — Davis, *Eloquent Animals,* p. 26

UNACCEPTABLE BORROWING OF PHRASES

Davis (1976) observed that the existence of a signing ape unsettled linguists and startled animal behaviorists (p. 26).

UNACCEPTABLE BORROWING OF STRUCTURE

Davis (1976) observed that if the presence of a sign-language-using chimp was disturbing for scientists studying language, it was also surprising to scientists studying animal behavior (p. 26).

To avoid plagiarizing an author's language, set the source aside, write from memory, and consult the source later to check for accuracy. This strategy prevents you from being captivated by the words on the page.

ACCEPTABLE PARAPHRASE

```
Davis (1976) observed that both linguists and
animal behaviorists were taken by surprise upon
learning of an ape's ability to use sign
language (p. 26).
```

35 | Integrating sources

The American Psychological Association recommends using past tense or present perfect verbs in phrases that introduce quotations: *Davis noted that* or *Davis has noted that* (not *Davis notes that*). Use the present tense only for discussing the results of an experiment (*the results show*) or knowledge that has clearly been established (*researchers agree*).

It is generally acceptable in the social sciences to call authors by their last name only, even on a first mention. If your paper refers to two authors with the same last name, use initials as well. In the references list, APA requires last names and initials (no first names).

35a. Integrating quotations

Readers need to move from your own words to the words of a source without feeling a jolt.

Using signal phrases.   Avoid dropping quotations into the text without warning. Instead, provide clear signal phrases, usually including the author's name and the date of publication, to prepare readers for the quotation.

DROPPED QUOTATION

```
Perhaps even more significant is the pattern that
Kanzi developed on his own in combining various
lexigrams. "When he gave an order combining two
symbols for action--such as 'chase' and 'hide'--
it was important for him that the first action--
'chase'--be done first" (Gibbons, 1991, p. 1561).
```

QUOTATION WITH SIGNAL PHRASE

```
Perhaps even more significant is the pattern that
Kanzi developed on his own in combining various
```

```
lexigrams. According to Gibbons (1991), "When he
gave an order combining two symbols for action--
such as 'chase' and 'hide'--it was important for
him that the first action--'chase'--be done
first" (p. 1561).
```

To avoid monotony, try to vary your signal phrases. The following models suggest a range of possibilities.

In the words of Terrace, ". . ."

As Davis has noted, ". . ."

The Gardners, Washoe's trainers, pointed out that ". . ."

". . .," claimed linguist Noam Chomsky.

". . .," wrote Eckholm, ". . ."

Psychologist H. S. Terrace has offered an odd argument for this view: ". . ."

Terrace answered these objections with the following analysis: ". . ."

When the signal phrase includes a verb, choose one that is appropriate in the context. Is your source arguing a point, making an observation, reporting a fact, drawing a conclusion, refuting an argument, or stating a belief? By choosing an appropriate verb, such as one on the following list, you can make your source's stance clear.

admitted	contended	reasoned
agreed	declared	refuted
argued	denied	rejected
asserted	emphasized	reported
believed	insisted	responded
claimed	noted	suggested
compared	observed	thought
confirmed	pointed out	wrote

It is not always necessary to quote full sentences from a source. At times you may wish to borrow only a phrase or to weave part of a source's sentence into your own sentence structure.

```
Bower (1988) reported that Kanzi practiced "simple
grammatical ordering rules," such as putting
actions before objects (p. 140).
```

```
Perhaps the best summation of the current state
of ape language studies comes from biologist
Robert Seyfarth (1982), who has concluded that
the line separating humans from other animals
"remains hazily drawn, somewhere between the word
and the sentence" (p. 18).
```

Using the ellipsis mark.   To condense a quoted passage, you can use the ellipsis mark (three periods, with spaces between) to indicate that you have omitted words. What remains must be grammatically complete.

```
Eckholm (1985) reported that "a 4-year-old pygmy
chimpanzee . . . has demonstrated what scientists
say are the most humanlike linguistic skills ever
documented in another animal" (p. A1).
```

The writer has omitted the words *at a research center near Atlanta,* which appeared in the original.

When you want to omit a full sentence or more, use a period before the three ellipsis dots.

```
According to Wade (1980), the horse Clever Hans
"could apparently count by tapping out numbers
with his hoof. . . . Clever Hans owes his
celebrity to his master's innocence. Von Osten
sincerely believed he had taught Hans to solve
arithmetical problems" (p. 1349).
```

Ordinarily, do not use an ellipsis mark at the beginning or at the end of a quotation. Readers will understand that the quoted material is taken from a longer passage. The only exception occurs when you fear that the author's meaning might be misinterpreted without ellipsis marks.

Using brackets.   Brackets (square parentheses) allow you to insert words of your own into quoted material, perhaps to explain a confusing reference or to keep a sentence grammatical in your context.

```
Seyfarth (1982) has written that "Premack [a
scientist at the University of Pennsylvania]
```

```
taught a seven-year-old chimpanzee, Sarah, that
the word for 'apple' was a small, plastic
triangle" (p. 13).
```

To indicate an error in a quotation, insert [sic] right after the error. Notice that the term *sic* is underlined and appears in brackets.

Setting off long quotations.   When you quote forty or more words, set off the quotation by indenting it one-half inch (or five spaces) from the left margin. Use the normal right margin and do not single-space.

Long quotations should be introduced by an informative sentence, usually followed by a colon. Quotation marks are unnecessary because the indented format tells readers that the words are taken directly from the source.

```
Desmond (1979) described how Washoe, when the
Gardners returned her to an ape colony in
Oklahoma, tried signing to the other apes:
     One particularly memorable day, a snake
     spread terror through the castaways on the
     ape island, and all but one fled in panic.
     This male sat absorbed, staring intently at
     the serpent. Then Washoe was seen running
     over signing to him "come, hurry up"
     (p. 42).
```

35b. Integrating summaries and paraphrases

Introduce most summaries and paraphrases with a signal phrase that mentions the author and date of publication and places the material in context. Readers will then understand where the summary or paraphrase begins.

Without the signal phrase (underlined) in the following example, readers might think that only the last sentence is being cited, when in fact the whole paragraph is based on the source.

```
     Recent studies at the Yerkes Primate Center
in Atlanta are breaking new ground. Researchers
```

Greenfield and Savage-Rumbaugh (1990) reported
that the pygmy chimp Kanzi seemed to understand
simple grammatical rules about lexigram order. For
instance, Kanzi learned that in two-word
utterances action precedes object, an ordering
also used by human children at the two-word
stage. What is impressive, said Greenfield and
Savage-Rumbaugh, is that in addition to being
semantically related, most of Kanzi's lexigram
combinations are original (p. 556).

There are times, however, when a signal phrase
naming the author is not necessary. Most readers will
understand, for example, that the citation at the end of
the following passage applies to the entire anecdote, not
just the last sentence.

One afternoon, Koko the gorilla, who was
often bored with language lessons, stubbornly and
repeatedly signaled "red" in American Sign
Language when asked the color of a white towel.
She did this even though she had correctly
identified the color white many times before. At
last the gorilla plucked a bit of red lint from
the towel and showed it to her trainer (Patterson
and Linden, 1981, pp. 80-81).

Notice that when there is no signal phrase naming the
author, the authors' names and the date must be included in the parentheses. Unless the work is short, also
include the page number in the parentheses.

35c. Integrating statistics and other facts

When you are citing a statistic or other specific fact, a
signal phrase is often not necessary. In most cases, readers will understand that the citation refers to the statistic or fact (not the whole paragraph).

By the age of ten, Kanzi had learned to
communicate about two hundred symbols on his
computerized board (Lewin, 1991, p. 51).

There is nothing wrong, however, with using a signal phrase.

```
Lewin (1991) reported that by the age of ten
Kanzi had learned to communicate about two
hundred symbols on his computerized board (p.
51).
```

36   APA documentation style

To document a source, the American Psychological Association (APA) recommends in-text citations that refer readers to a list of references. APA's most recent guidelines appear in the *Publication Manual of the American Psychological Association,* 5th ed. (2001).

36a. APA in-text citations

The APA's in-text citations provide at least the author's last name and the date of publication. For direct quotations, a page number is given as well.

NOTE: In the models that follow, notice that APA style requires the use of the past tense or the present perfect tense in signal phrases introducing material that has been cited: *Smith reported, Smith has argued.*

1. A QUOTATION. Ordinarily, introduce the quotation with a signal phrase that includes the author's last name followed by the date of publication in parentheses. Put the page number (preceded by "p.") in parentheses at the end of the quotation.

As Davis (1978) reported, "If the existence of a signing ape was unsettling for linguists, it was also startling news for animal behaviorists" (p. 26).

When the author's name does not appear in the signal phrase, place the author's last name, the date, and the page number in parentheses at the end: (Hart, 1996, p. 109).

2. A SUMMARY OR A PARAPHRASE. For a summary or a paraphrase, include the author's last name and the date either in a signal phrase or in parentheses at the end. For short works a page number is not required, but APA advises including a page number if it would help readers find a specific passage in a book or long article.

According to Hart (1996), researchers took Terrace's conclusions seriously, and funding for language experiments soon declined (p. 40).

Researchers took Terrace's conclusions seriously, and funding for language experiments soon declined (Hart, 1996, p. 40).

3. TWO AUTHORS. Name both authors in the signal phrase or parentheses each time you cite the work. In the parentheses, use "&" between the authors' names: (Patterson & Linden, 1981). In the signal phrase, use "and."

Patterson and Linden (1981) agreed that the gorilla Koko acquired language more slowly than a normal speaking child.

Koko acquired language more slowly than a normal speaking child (Patterson & Linden, 1981).

4. THREE TO FIVE AUTHORS. Identify all authors in the signal phrase or parentheses the first time you cite the source:

(Levy, Bertrand, Muller, Vining, & Majors, 1997). In subsequent citations, use the first author's name followed by "et al." (Latin for "and others") in either the signal phrase or the parentheses: (Levy et al., 1997).

5. SIX OR MORE AUTHORS.   Use only the first author's name followed by "et al." in all citations: (Blili et al., 1996).

6. CORPORATE AUTHOR.   If the author is a government agency or other corporate organization with a long and cumbersome name, spell out the name the first time you use it in a citation, followed by an abbreviation in brackets. In later citations, simply use the abbreviation.

FIRST CITATION   `(National Institute of Mental Health [NIMH], 2000).`

LATER CITATIONS   `(NIMH, 2000).`

7. UNKNOWN AUTHOR.   If the author is not given, either use the complete title in a signal phrase or use the first word or two of the title in the parenthetical citation: ("Innovations," 1997). Titles of articles appear in quotation marks; titles of books are italicized.

   If "Anonymous" is specified as the author, treat it as if it were a real name: (Anonymous, 2000). In the list of references, also use the name Anonymous as the author.

8. AUTHORS WITH THE SAME LAST NAME.   To avoid confusion, use initials with the last names if your list of references contains two or more authors with the same last name: (D. L. Johnson, 1996).

9. PERSONAL COMMUNICATION.   Conversations, memos, letters, e-mail, and similar unpublished person-to-person communications should be cited by initials, last name, and precise date: (F. Moore, personal communication, January 4, 2000). Do not include personal communications in the list of references.

10. AN ELECTRONIC DOCUMENT.   Cite an electronic document as you would any other document (using the author-date style).

`R. Fouts and D. Fouts (1999) have explained one benefit of ape language research: It has shown us how to teach children with linguistic disabilities.`

11. TWO OR MORE WORKS IN THE SAME PARENTHESES.   When your parenthetical citation names two or more works, put them in the same order that they appear in the list of references, separated by semicolons: (Gilbert, 1995; Leira, 1994).

36b. APA list of references

In APA style, the alphabetical list of works cited is titled "References." Following are models illustrating the form that APA recommends for entries in the list of references. Observe all details: capitalization, punctuation, italicizing, and so on. For advice on preparing the references page, see pages 163–64. For a sample references page, see page 167.

NOTE: APA recommends using a hanging indent, as shown in this section, in the list of references (see also page 163).

Books

1. BASIC FORMAT FOR A BOOK

Tapscott, D. (1998). *Growing up digital.* New
    York: McGraw-Hill.

2. MULTIPLE AUTHORS

Hamer, D., & Copeland, P. (1998). *Living with our
    genes: Why they matter more than you think.*
    New York: Doubleday.

Winncott, D. W., Shepherd, R., Johns, J., &
    Robinson, H. T. (1996). *Thinking about
    children.* Reading, MA: Addison-Wesley.

3. CORPORATE AUTHOR

Bank of Boston. (1997). *Banking by remote
    control.* Boston: Author.

4. UNKNOWN AUTHOR

Oxford essential world atlas. (1996). New York:
    Oxford University Press.

5. EDITORS

Duncan, G. J., & Brooks-Gunn, J. (Eds.). (1997).
    Consequences of growing up poor. New York:
    Russell Sage Foundation.

6. TRANSLATION

Singer, I. B. (1998). *Shadows on the Hudson*
    (J. Sherman, Trans.). New York: Farrar, Straus
    and Giroux. (Original work published 1957)

7. EDITION OTHER THAN THE FIRST

Helfer, M. E., Kempe, R. S., & Krugman, R. D.
    (1997). *The battered child* (5th ed.).
    Chicago: University of Chicago Press.

8. ARTICLE IN AN EDITED BOOK

Fesmire, S. (1997). The social basis of
    character: An ecological humanist approach.
    In H. LaFollette (Ed.). *Ethics in practice*
    (pp. 282-292). Cambridge, MA: Blackwell.

9. MULTIVOLUME WORK

Golden, R. (Ed.). (1999). *The social dimension of
    Western civilization* (Vols. 1-2). Boston:
    Bedford.

10. ONE VOLUME OF A MULTIVOLUME WORK

Golden, R. (Ed.). (1999). *The social dimension of
    Western civilization* (Vol. 2). Boston:
    Bedford.

Articles in periodicals

11. ARTICLE IN A MAGAZINE

Kadrey, R. (1998, March). Carbon copy: Meet the
    first human clone. *Wired, 6,* 146-150, 180,
    220.

12. ARTICLE IN A NEWSPAPER

Haney, D. Q. (1998, February 20). Finding eats at
    mystery of appetite. *The Oregonian,* pp. A1,
    A17.

13. ARTICLE IN A JOURNAL PAGINATED BY VOLUME

McLoyd, V. C. (1998). Socioeconomic disadvantage
    and child development. *American Psychologist,
    53,* 185-204.

14. ARTICLE IN A JOURNAL PAGINATED BY ISSUE

Roberts, P. (1998). The new food anxiety.
    Psychology Today, 31(2), 30-38, 74.

15. UNSIGNED ARTICLE IN A PERIODICAL

EMFs on the brain. (1995, January 21). *Science
    News, 141,* 44.

16. REVIEW

Ehrenhalt, A. (1997, February 10). [Review of the
    book *Virtuous reality*]. *The Weekly Standard,*
    pp. 31-34.

17. LETTER TO THE EDITOR

Westberg, L. (1997). South Bronx, New York
    [Letter to the editor]. *Orion, 16*(1), 4.

Electronic Sources

18. ARTICLE FROM AN ONLINE PERIODICAL. If the article appears in a printed journal, a URL is not required; instead, include "Electronic version" in brackets after the title of the article.

Williams, S. L., Brakke, K. E., & Savage-Rumbaugh,
    E. S. (1977). Comprehension skills of
    language-competent and nonlanguage-competent
    apes [Electronic version]. *Language and
    Communication, 17*(4), 301-317.

If there is no print version, include the date you accessed the source and the article's URL.

Ashe, D. D., & McCutcheon, L. E. (2001, May 4).
    Shyness, loneliness, and attitude toward
    celebritites, *Current Research in Social
    Psychology, 6*(9). Retrieved July 3, 2001,
    from http://www.uiowa.edu/~grpproc/crisp/
    crisp.6.9.htm

NOTE: When you have retrieved an article from a newspaper's searchable Web site, give the URL for the site, not for the exact source.

Cary, B. (2001, June 18). Mentors of the mind.
    Los Angeles Times. Retrieved July 5, 2001,
    from http://www.latimes.com

19. ARTICLE FROM A DATABASE

Holliday, R. E., & Hayes, B. K. (2001, January).
    Dissociating automatic and international
    processes in children's eyewitness memory.
    *Journal of Experimental Child Psychology,
    75*(1), 1-5. Retrieved February 21, 2001, from
    Expanded Academic ASAP database (A59317972).

20. NONPERIODICAL WEB DOCUMENT

Cain, A., & Burris, M. (1999, April). *Investigation
    of the use of mobile phones while driving.*
    Retrieved January 15, 2000, from http://www
    .cutr.eng.usf.edu/its/mobile_phone_text.htm

21. CHAPTER OR SECTION IN A WEB DOCUMENT

Heuer, R. J., Jr. (1999). Keeping an open mind. In
    Psychology of intelligence analysis (chap. 6).
    Retrieved July 7, 2001, from http://www.cia
    .gov/csi/books/19104/art9.html

22. E-MAIL. E-mail messages are personal communications and are not included in the list of references.

23. COMPUTER PROGRAM

Kaufmann, W. J., III, & Comins, N. F. (1998).
    Discovering the universe (Version 4.1)
    [Computer software]. New York: W. H. Freeman.

Other sources

24. DISSERTATION ABSTRACT

Hu, X. (1996). Consumption and social inequality
    in urban Guangdong, China (Doctoral
    dissertation. University of Hawaii, 1996).
    Dissertation Abstracts International, 57,
    3280A.

25. GOVERNMENT DOCUMENT

U.S. Bureau of the Census. (1996). *Statistical
    abstract of the United States* (116th ed.).
    Washington, DC: U.S. Government Printing
    Office.

26. CONFERENCE PROCEEDINGS

Schnase, J. L., & Cunnius, E. L. (Eds.). (1995).
*Proceedings of CSCL '95: The First
International Conference on Computer Support
for Collaborative Learning*. Mahwah, NJ:
Erlbaum.

27. MOTION PICTURE

Soderbergh, S. (Director). (2000). *Traffic* [Motion
picture]. United States: Gramercy Pictures.

37 APA manuscript format

The American Psychological Association makes the following recommendations for formatting a manuscript.

Materials and typeface. Use good-quality 8½" × 11" white paper. For a paper typed on a computer, make sure that the print quality meets your instructor's standards. Avoid a typeface that is unusual or hard to read.

Title page. Begin a college paper with a title page. Type the page number, flush right (against the right margin), one-half inch from the top of the page. Before the page number type a short title, consisting of the first two or three words of your title.

The APA manual does not provide guidelines for the placement of certain information necessary for college papers, but most instructors will want you to supply a title page similar to the one on page 165.

Margins, spacing, and indentation. Use margins of one inch on all sides of the page. If you are working on a computer, do not justify the right margin.

Double-space throughout the paper, and indent the first line of each paragraph one-half inch (or five spaces).

For quotations longer than forty words, indent each line one-half inch (or five spaces) from the left margin. Double-space between the body of the paper and the quotation, and double-space between lines in the quotation. Quotation marks are not needed when a quotation is indented. (See also p. 151.)

Page numbers and short title. In the upper right-hand corner of each page, one-half inch from the top of the page, type the page number, preceded by the short title that you typed on the title page. Number all pages, including the title page.

Punctuation and typing. APA guidelines call for one space after all punctuation. To form a dash, type two hyphens with no space between them. Do not put a space on either side of the dash.

Abstract. If your instructor requires one, include an abstract right after the title page. Center the word "Abstract" one inch from the top of the page; double-space the text of the abstract as you do the body of your paper.

An abstract is a 75-to-100-word paragraph that provides readers with a quick overview of your essay. It should express your thesis (or central idea) and your key points; it should also briefly suggest any implications or applications of the research you discuss in the paper.

Headings. Although headings are not necessary, their use is encouraged in the social sciences. For most undergraduate papers, use no more than one or two levels of headings. Major headings should be centered, with the first letter of important words capitalized; minor words — articles, short prepositions, and coordinating conjunctions — are not capitalized unless they are the first word. Subheadings should be typed flush left (against the left margin) and italicized; the rules on capitalization are the same as for major headings.

Visuals. The APA classifies visuals as tables and figures (figures include graphs, charts, drawings, and photographs). Keep visuals as simple as possible. Label each clearly — Table 1, Figure 3, and so on — and include a caption that concisely describes its subject. In the text of your paper, discuss the most significant features of each visual. Ask your instructor for guidelines on placement of visuals in the paper.

Preparing the "References" page

On page 167 is a sample list of references in the APA style. This list, titled "References," begins on a new page at the end of the paper.

In the upper right corner of the page, type the short title of your paper followed by five spaces and the page number. Center the heading "References" (without quotation marks) one inch from the top of the page. Double-space throughout.

Indenting. APA recommends using hanging indents, which highlight the authors' names and thus make it easy for readers to scan through the alphabetized list of references. To create a hanging indent, type the first line of an entry flush left and indent any additional lines one-half inch (or five spaces), as shown here.

```
Stoessinger, J. G. (1998). Why nations go to war
     (7th ed.). New York: St. Martin's Press.
```

Some instructors may prefer a paragraph-style indent, as in the following example.

```
     Stoessinger, J. G. (1998). Why nations go to
war (7th ed.). New York: St. Martin's Press.
```

Alphabetizing the list. Alphabetize your list by the last names of the authors (or editors); when the author or editor is unknown, alphabetize by the first word of the title other than *A, An,* and *The.*

If your list includes two or more works by the same author, arrange the entries by date, the earliest first. If your list includes two or more articles by the same author in the same year, arrange them alphabetically by title. Add lowercase letters beginning with "a," "b," and so on, within the parentheses immediately following the year: (1997a, July 7).

Authors and dates. Invert *all* authors' names and use initials instead of first names. With two or more authors, use an ampersand (&). Separate the names with commas. Include names for the first six authors; if there are additional authors, end the list with "et al." (Latin for "and others").

After the names of the authors, place the date in parentheses.

Titles of books and articles.   Italicize the titles and subtitles of books; capitalize only the first word of the title and subtitle (as well as all proper nouns).

Do not place titles of articles in quotation marks, and capitalize only the first word of the title and subtitle (and all proper nouns). Capitalize names of periodicals as you would capitalize them ordinarily. (See section 22.)

The abbreviation "p." (or "pp.").   Abbreviations for "page" or "pages" are used before page numbers of newspaper articles and articles in edited books but not before page numbers of articles appearing in magazines and scholarly journals.

NOTE: The sample references page (see p. 167) shows you how to type your list of references. For information about the exact format of each entry in your list, consult the models in section 36b.

Apes and Language   1

Apes and Language:

A Review of the Literature

Karen Shaw

Psychology 110, Section 2

Professor Verdi

April 5, 2001

Apes and Language:

A Review of the Literature

Over the past twenty-five years, researchers have demonstrated that the great apes (chimpanzees, gorillas, and orangutans) resemble humans in language abilities more than had been thought possible. Just how far that resemblance extends, however, has been a matter of some controversy. Researchers agree that apes have acquired fairly large vocabularies in American Sign Language and in artificial languages, but they have drawn quite different conclusions in addressing the following questions: (1) How spontaneously have apes used language? (2) How creatively have apes used language? (3) To what extent can apes create sentences? (4) What are some implications of the ape language studies? This review of the literature focuses on these four questions.

How Spontaneously

Have Apes Used Language?

In an influential article, Terrace, Petitto, Sanders, and Bever (1979) argued that the apes in language experiments were not using language spontaneously, that they were merely imitating their trainers, responding to conscious or unconscious cues. Terrace and his colleagues at Columbia University had trained a chimpanzee, Nim, in American Sign Language, so their skepticism about the apes' abilities received much attention. In fact, funding for ape language research was sharply reduced following publication of their 1979 article "Can an Ape Create a Sentence?"

Apes and Language   16

References

Begley, S. (1998, January 19). Aping language. *Newsweek, 131,* 56-58.

Davis, F. (1978). *Eloquent animals: A study in animal communication.* New York: Coward, McCann & Geoghegan.

Eckholm, E. (1985a, June 25). Kanzi the chimp: A life in science. *The New York Times,* pp. C1, C3.

Eckholm, E. (1985b, June 24). Pygmy chimp readily learns language skill. *The New York Times,* pp. A1, B7.

Greenfield, P. M., & Savage-Rumbaugh, E. S. (1990). Grammatical combination in *Pan paniscus:* Processes of learning and invention in the evolution and development of language. In S. T. Parker & K. R. Gibson (Eds.), *"Language" and intelligence in monkeys and apes: Comparative developmental perspectives* (pp. 540-578). Cambridge: Cambridge University Press.

Johnson, G. (1995, June 6). Chimp talk debate: Is it really language? *The New York Times.* Retrieved February 2, 1998, from http://www.nytimes.com

Leakey, R., & Lewin, R. (1992). *Origins reconsidered: In search of what makes us human.* New York: Doubleday.

Lewin, R. (1991, April 29). Look who's talking now. *New Scientist, 130,* 49-52.

Patterson, F., & Linden, E. (1981). *The education of Koko.* New York: Holt, Rinehart & Winston.

Terrace, H. S., Petitto, L. A., Sanders, R. J., & Bever, T. G. (1979). Can an ape create a sentence? *Science, 206,* 891-902.

CHICAGO

Chicago-Style Papers

Most assignments in history and other humanities classes are based to some extent on reading. At times you will be asked to respond to one or two readings, such as essays or historical documents. At other times you may be asked to write a research paper that draws on a wide variety of sources.

Most history instructors and some humanities instructors require the *Chicago*-style footnotes or endnotes explained in section 41. When you write a paper that is based on sources, you face three main challenges: (1) supporting a thesis, (2) documenting sources and avoiding plagiarism, and (3) integrating quotations and other source material.

38 Supporting a thesis

Most assignments ask you to form a thesis, or main idea, and to support that thesis with well-organized evidence.

38a. Finding a thesis

A thesis is a one-sentence (or occasionally a two-sentence) statement of your central idea. Usually your thesis will appear at the end of the first paragraph (as in the example on p. 192), but if you need to provide readers with considerable background information, you may place it in the second paragraph.

Although the thesis appears early in your paper, do not attempt to write it until fairly late in your reading and writing process. Early in the process, you can keep your mind open—yet focused—by posing questions. The thesis that you articulate later in the process will be a reasoned answer to the central question you pose, as in the following example.

RESEARCH QUESTION

To what extent was Confederate Major General Nathan Bedford Forrest responsible for the massacre of Union troops at Fort Pillow?

POSSIBLE THESIS

Although we will never know whether Nathan Bedford Forrest directly ordered the massacre of Union troops at Fort Pillow, evidence suggests that he was responsible for it.

Notice that the thesis expresses a view on a debatable issue—an issue about which intelligent, well-meaning people might disagree. The writer's job is to convince such readers that this view is worth taking seriously.

38b. Organizing your evidence

The body of your paper will consist of evidence in support of your thesis. Instead of getting tangled up in a complex, formal outline, sketch an informal plan that organizes your evidence in bold strokes. The student who wrote about Fort Pillow used a simple list of questions as the blueprint for his paper. In the paper itself, these became headings that helped readers follow the writer's line of argument.

What happened at Fort Pillow?

Did Forrest order the massacre?

Can Forrest be held responsible for the massacre?

39   Citing sources; avoiding plagiarism

In researched writing, you will be drawing on the work of other writers, and you must document their contributions by citing your sources. Sources are cited for two reasons: to tell readers where your information comes from and to give credit to the writers from whom you have borrowed words and ideas. To borrow another writer's language or ideas without proper acknowledgment is a form of dishonesty known as *plagiarism*.

39a. Citing sources

Citations are required when you quote from a source, when you summarize or paraphrase a source, and when you borrow facts and ideas (except for common knowledge). (See also section 39b.)

Chicago citations consist of numbered notes in the text of the paper that refer readers to notes with corresponding numbers either at the foot of the page (footnotes) or at the end of the paper (endnotes).

TEXT

Governor John Andrew was not allowed to recruit black soldiers from out of state. "Ostensibly," writes Peter Burchard, "no recruiting was done outside Massachusetts, but it was an open secret that Andrew's agents were working far and wide."[1]

NOTE

1. Peter Burchard, One Gallant Rush: Robert Gould Shaw and His Brave Black Regiment (New York: St. Martin's Press, 1965), 85.

For detailed advice on using *Chicago*-style notes, see 41. When you use footnotes or endnotes, you will usually need to provide a bibliography as well. (See 41b.)

39b. Avoiding plagiarism

Your research paper is a collaboration between you and your sources. To be fair and ethical, you must acknowledge your debt to the writers of these sources. If you don't, you are guilty of plagiarism, a serious academic offense.

Three different acts are considered plagiarism: (1) failing to cite quotations and borrowed ideas, (2) failing to enclose borrowed language in quotation marks, and (3) failing to put summaries and paraphrases in your own words.

Citing quotations and borrowed ideas.   You must of course cite the source of all direct quotations. You must also cite any ideas borrowed from a source: paraphrases of sentences, summaries of paragraphs or chapters, statistics and little-known facts, and tables, graphs, or diagrams.

The only exception is common knowledge — information that your readers could find in any number of general sources because it is commonly known. For example, the current population of the United States is common knowledge in such fields as sociology and economics; Freud's theory of the unconscious is common knowledge in the field of psychology.

As a rule, when you have seen certain information repeatedly in your reading, you don't need to cite it. However, when information has appeared in only one or two sources or when it is controversial, you should cite it. If a topic is new to you and you are not sure what is considered common knowledge or what is a matter of controversy, ask someone with expertise. When in doubt, cite the source.

Enclosing borrowed language in quotation marks. To indicate that you are using a source's exact phrases or sentences, you must enclose them in quotation marks unless they have been set off from the text by indenting. (See p. 177.) To omit the quotation marks is to claim — falsely — that the language is your own. Such an omission is plagiarism even if you have cited the source.

ORIGINAL SOURCE

For many Southerners it was psychologically impossible to see a black man bearing arms as anything but an incipient slave uprising complete with arson, murder, pillage, and rapine.

> —Dudley Taylor Cornish, *The Sable Arm:
> Negro Troops in the Union Army,
> 1861–1865,* p. 158

PLAGIARISM

According to Civil War historian Dudley Taylor Cornish, for many Southerners it was psychologically impossible to see a black man bearing arms as anything but an incipient slave uprising complete with arson, murder, pillage, and rapine.[2]

BORROWED LANGUAGE IN QUOTATION MARKS

According to Civil War historian Dudley Taylor Cornish, "For many Southerners it was psychologically impossible to see a black man bearing arms as anything but an incipient slave uprising complete with arson, murder, pillage, and rapine."[2]

Putting summaries and paraphrases in your own words. When you summarize or paraphrase, you must restate the source's meaning using your own language. In the following example, the paraphrase is plagiarized—even though the source is cited—because too much of its language is borrowed from the source without quotation marks. The underlined phrases have been copied word-for-word. In addition, the writer has closely followed the sentence structure of the original source, merely plugging in some synonyms (such as *fifty percent* for *half* and *savage hatred* for *fierce, bitter animosity*).

ORIGINAL SOURCE

Half of the force holding Fort Pillow were Negroes, former slaves now enrolled in the Union Army. Toward them Forrest's troops had the fierce, bitter animosity of men who had been educated to regard the colored race as inferior and who for the first time had encountered that race armed and fighting against white men. The sight enraged and perhaps terrified many of the Confederates and aroused in them the ugly spirit of a lynching mob.

— Albert Castel, "The Fort Pillow Massacre," pp. 46–47

PLAGIARISM: UNACCEPTABLE BORROWING

Albert Castel suggests that much of the brutality at Fort Pillow can be traced to racial attitudes. Fifty percent of the troops holding Fort Pillow were Negroes, former slaves who had joined the Union Army. Toward them Forrest's soldiers displayed the savage hatred of men who had been taught the inferiority of blacks and who for the first time had confronted them armed and fighting against white men. The vision angered and perhaps frightened the Confederates and aroused in them the ugly spirit of a lynching mob.[3]

To avoid plagiarizing an author's language, set the source aside, write from memory, and consult the source later to check for accuracy. This strategy prevents you from being captivated by the words on the page.

ACCEPTABLE PARAPHRASE

```
Albert Castel suggests that much of the brutality
at Fort Pillow can be traced to racial attitudes.
Nearly half of the Union troops were blacks, men
whom the Confederates had been raised to consider
their inferiors. The shock and perhaps fear of
facing armed ex-slaves in battle for the first
time may well have unleashed the fury that led to
the massacre.[3]
```

40 Integrating sources

When using the *Chicago* style of documentation, use present tense or present perfect tense verbs in phrases that introduce quotations or other source material from nonfiction sources: *Foote points out that* or *Foote has pointed out that* (not *Foote pointed out that*). If you have good reason to emphasize that the author's language or opinion was articulated in the past, however, the past tense is acceptable.

The first time you mention an author, use the full name: *Shelby Foote argues.* . . . When you refer to the author again, you may use the last name only: *Foote raises an important question.*

40a. Integrating quotations

Readers should be able to move from your own words to the words you quote from a source without feeling a jolt.

Using signal phrases. Avoid dropping quotations into the text without warning. Instead, provide clear signal phrases, usually including the author's name, to prepare readers for the source.

DROPPED QUOTATION

```
Not surprisingly, those testifying on the Union
and Confederate sides recalled events at Fort Pil-
```

low quite differently. Unionists claimed that
their troops had abandoned their arms and were in
full retreat. "The Confederates, however, all
agreed that the Union troops retreated to the
river with arms in their hands."[4]

QUOTATION WITH SIGNAL PHRASE

Not surprisingly, those testifying on the Union
and Confederate sides recalled events at Fort
Pillow quite differently. Unionists claimed that
their troops had abandoned their arms and were in
full retreat. "The Confederates, however," writes
historian Albert Castel, "all agreed that the
Union troops retreated to the river with arms in
their hands."[4]

To avoid monotony, try to vary your signal phrases.
The following models suggest a range of possibilities.

In the words of historian James M. McPherson, ". . ."

As Dudley Taylor Cornish has argued, ". . ."

In a letter to his wife, a Confederate soldier who wit-
nessed the massacre wrote that ". . ."

". . .," claims Benjamin Quarles.

". . .," writes Albert Castel, ". . ."

Shelby Foote offers an intriguing interpretation of
these events:

When the signal phrase includes a verb, choose one
that is appropriate in the context. Is your source arguing a point, making an observation, reporting a fact, refuting an argument, or stating a belief? By choosing an
appropriate verb, such as one on the following list, you
can make your source's stance clear.

admits	compares	insists	rejects
agrees	confirms	notes	reports
argues	contends	observes	responds
asserts	declares	points out	suggests
believes	denies	reasons	thinks
claims	emphasizes	refutes	writes

It is not always necessary to quote full sentences
from a source. At times you may wish to borrow only a

phrase or to weave part of a source's sentence into your
own sentence structure.

As Hurst has pointed out, until there was "an
outcry in the northern press," even the Confederates did not deny that there had been a massacre
at Fort Pillow.[5]

Union surgeon Dr. Charles Fitch testified that
after being taken prisoner by Forrest he saw
Southern soldiers "kill every Negro who made his
appearance in Federal uniform."[6]

Using the ellipsis mark.   To condense a quoted passage,
you can use the ellipsis mark (three periods, with spaces
between) to indicate that you have omitted words. The
sentence that remains must be grammatically complete.

Union surgeon Fitch's testimony that all women
and children had been evacuated from Fort Pillow
before the attack conflicts with Forrest's report:
"We captured . . . about 40 negro women and
children."[7]

The writer has omitted several words not relevant to the
issue at hand: *164 Federals, 75 negro troops, and.*
    When you want to omit a full sentence or more, use
a period before the three ellipsis dots. For an example,
see the long quotation on page 177.
    Ordinarily, do not use an ellipsis mark at the be-
ginning or at the end of a quotation. Readers will understand that the quoted material is taken from a longer
passage.

Using brackets.   Brackets allow you to insert words of
your own into quoted material, perhaps to explain a confusing reference or to keep a sentence grammatical in
your context.

According to Albert Castel, "It can be reasonably
argued that he [Forrest] was justified in believ-
ing that the approaching steamships intended to
aid the garrison [at Fort Pillow]."[8]

NOTE: Use [*sic*] to indicate that an error in a quoted sentence appears in the original source. (An example appears in the long quotation below.) However, if a source is filled with errors, as is the case with many historical documents, this use of [*sic*] can become distracting and is best avoided.

Setting off long quotations.   *Chicago* style allows you some leeway in deciding whether to set off a quotation or run it into your text. For emphasis you may want to set off a quotation of more than four or five lines of text; almost certainly you should set off quotations of ten lines or more. To set off a quotation, indent it one-half inch (or five spaces) from the left margin and use the normal right margin. Double-space the indented quotation.

Long quotations should be introduced by an informative sentence, usually followed by a colon. Quotation marks are unnecessary because the indented format tells readers that the words are taken directly from the source.

In a letter home, Confederate officer Achilles V. Clark recounted what happened at Fort Pillow:

> Words cannot describe the scene. The poor deluded negroes would run up to our men fall upon their knees and with uplifted hands scream for mercy but they were ordered to their feet and then shot down. The whitte [*sic*] men fared but little better. . . . I with several others tried to stop the butchery and at one time had partially succeeded, but Gen. Forrest ordered them shot down like dogs, and the carnage continued.[9]

40b. Integrating summaries and paraphrases

Introduce most summaries and paraphrases with a signal phrase that names the author and places the material in context. Readers will then understand that everything between the signal phrase and the numbered note summarizes or paraphrases the cited source.

Without the signal phrase (underlined) in the following example, readers might think that only the last sentence is being cited, when in fact the whole paragraph is based on the source.

<u>According to Kenneth Davis</u>, official Confederate policy was that black soldiers were to be treated as runaway slaves; in addition, the Confederate Congress decreed that white Union officers commanding black troops be killed. Confederate Lieutenant General Kirby Smith of Mississippi boldly announced that he would kill all captured black troops. Smith's policy never met with strong opposition from the Richmond government.[10]

40c. Integrating statistics and other facts

When you are citing a statistic or other specific fact, a signal phrase is often not necessary. In most cases, readers will understand that the citation refers to the statistic or fact (not the whole paragraph).

Of the 295 white troops garrisoned at Fort Pillow, 168 were taken prisoner. Black troops fared much worse, with only 58 of 262 men being taken into custody.[11]

There is nothing wrong, however, with using a signal phrase.

Shelby Foote notes that of the 295 white troops garrisoned at Fort Pillow, 168 were taken prisoner but that black troops fared much worse, with only 58 of 262 men being taken into custody.[11]

41   *Chicago* documentation style (footnotes or endnotes)

Professors in history and some humanities often require footnotes or endnotes based on *The Chicago Manual of Style,* 14th ed. (Chicago: U of Chicago P, 1993). When you use *Chicago*-style notes, you will usually be asked to include a bibliography at the end of your paper. (See 41b.)

41a. First and subsequent references to a source

The first time you cite a source, the note should include publishing information for that work as well as the page number on which the specific quotation, paraphrase, or summary may be found.

```
    1. Peter Burchard, One Gallant Rush: Robert
Gould Shaw and His Brave Black Regiment (New
York: St. Martin's Press, 1965), 85.
```

For subsequent references to a source you have already cited, you may simply give the author's last name, followed by a comma and the page or pages cited.

```
    2. Burchard, 31.
```

If you cite more than one work by the same author, include a short form of the title in subsequent citations. A short form of the title of a book is underlined or italicized; a short form of the title of an article is put in quotation marks.

```
    2. Burchard, One Gallant Rush, 31.

    4. Burchard, "Civil War," 10.
```

NOTE: *Chicago* style no longer requires the use of "ibid." to refer to the work cited in the previous note. The Latin abbreviations "op. cit." and "loc. cit." are no longer used.

41b. *Chicago*-style bibliography

A bibliography, which appears at the end of your paper, lists every work you have cited in your notes; in addition, it may include works that you consulted but did not cite. For advice on constructing the list, see page 190. A sample bibliography appears on page 194.

41c. Model notes and bibliographic entries

The following models are consistent with guidelines set forth in *The Chicago Manual of Style,* 14th ed. For each type of source, a model note appears first, followed by a model bibliographic entry. The model note shows the format you should use when citing a source for the first time. For subsequent citations of a source, use shortened notes (see section 41a).

Books

1. BASIC FORMAT FOR A BOOK

   1. Robert Service, A History of Twentieth-Century Russia (Cambridge: Harvard University Press, 1998), 314-30.

Service, Robert. A History of Twentieth-Century Russia. Cambridge: Harvard University Press, 1998.

2. TWO OR THREE AUTHORS

   2. Rudolph O. de la Garza, Z. Anthony Kruszewski, and Tomás A. Arciniega, Chicanos and Native Americans: The Territorial Minorities (Englewood Cliffs, N.J.: Prentice-Hall, 1973), 8.

Garza, Rudolph O. de la, Z. Anthony Kruszewski, and Tomás A. Arciniega. Chicanos and Native Americans: The Territorial Minorities. Englewood Cliffs, N.J.: Prentice-Hall, 1973.

3. FOUR OR MORE AUTHORS

   3. Gary B. Nash et al., The American People, 4th ed. (New York: Addison Wesley Longman, 1998), 164.

Nash, Gary B., et al. The American People. 4th ed. New York: Addison Wesley Longman, 1998.

4. UNKNOWN AUTHOR

   4. The Men's League Handbook on Women's Suffrage (London, 1912), 23.

The Men's League Handbook on Women's Suffrage.
London, 1912.

5. AUTHOR'S NAME IN TITLE

5. *Long Walk to Freedom: The Autobiography of
Nelson Mandela* (Boston: Little, Brown, 1995), 435.

Mandela, Nelson. *Long Walk to Freedom: The
Autobiography of Nelson Mandela.* Boston:
Little, Brown, 1995.

6. EDITED WORK WITHOUT AN AUTHOR

6. Marshall Sklare, ed., *Understanding American Jewry* (New Brunswick, N.J.: Transaction Books,
1982), 49.

Sklare, Marshall, ed. *Understanding American
Jewry.* New Brunswick, N.J.: Transaction
Books, 1982.

7. EDITED WORK WITH AN AUTHOR

7. William L. Riordon, *Plunkitt of Tammany
Hall,* ed. Terrence J. McDonald (Boston: Bedford
Books, 1994), 33.

Riordon, William L. *Plunkitt of Tammany Hall.*
Edited by Terrence J. McDonald. Boston:
Bedford Books, 1994.

8. TRANSLATED WORK

8. Gabriel García Márquez, *News of a Kidnapping,* trans. Edith Grossman (New York: Knopf,
1997), 154-67.

García Márquez, Gabriel. *News of a Kidnapping.*
Translated by Edith Grossman. New York:
Knopf, 1997.

9. EDITION OTHER THAN THE FIRST

9. Andrew F. Rolle, *California: A History,*
5th ed. (Wheeling, Ill.: Harlan Davidson, 1998),
243-46.

Rolle, Andrew F. <u>California: A History</u>. 5th ed.
　　　Wheeling, Ill.: Harlan Davidson, 1998.

10. UNTITLED VOLUME IN A MULTIVOLUME WORK

　　　10. <u>New Cambridge Modern History</u> (Cambridge:
Cambridge University Press, 1957), 1:52-53.

<u>New Cambridge Modern History</u>. Vol. 1. Cambridge:
　　　Cambridge University Press, 1957.

11. TITLED VOLUME IN A MULTIVOLUME WORK

　　　11. Horst Boog et al., <u>The Attack on the So-</u>
<u>viet Union</u>, vol. 4 of <u>Germany and the Second</u>
<u>World War</u> (Cambridge: Oxford University Press,
1998), 70-72.

Boog, Horst, et al. <u>The Attack on the Soviet</u>
　　　<u>Union</u>. Vol. 4 of <u>Germany and the Second</u>
　　　<u>World War</u>. Cambridge: Oxford University
　　　Press, 1998.

12. WORK IN AN ANTHOLOGY

　　　12. Roland Barthes, "The Discourse of
History," in <u>The Postmodern History Reader</u>, ed.
Keith Jenkins (New York: Routledge, 1997), 121.

Barthes, Roland. "The Discourse of History." In
　　　<u>The Postmodern History Reader</u>, edited by
　　　Keith Jenkins. New York: Routledge, 1997.

13. LETTER IN A PUBLISHED COLLECTION

　　　13. James Thurber to Harold Ross, 27 December
1948, <u>Selected Letters of James Thurber</u>, ed.
Helen Thurber and Edward Weeks (Boston: Little,
Brown, 1981), 65-66.

Thurber, James. Letter to Harold Ross, 27
　　　December 1948. In <u>Selected Letters of James</u>
　　　<u>Thurber</u>, edited by Helen Thurber and Edward
　　　Weeks, 65-66. Boston: Little, Brown, 1981.

14. WORK IN A SERIES

　　　14. Robert M. Laughlin, <u>Of Cabbages and</u>
<u>Kings: Tales from Zinacantán</u>, Smithsonian Contri-

butions to Anthropology, vol. 23 (Washington, D.C.: Smithsonian Institution Press, 1977), 14.

Laughlin, Robert M. <u>Of Cabbages and Kings: Tales from Zinacantán</u>. Smithsonian Contributions to Anthropology, vol. 23. Washington, D.C.: Smithsonian Institution Press, 1977.

15. ENCYCLOPEDIA OR DICTIONARY

15. <u>Encyclopaedia Britannica</u>, 15th ed., s.v. "evolution."

NOTE: The abbreviation "s.v." is for the Latin *sub verbo* ("under the word").

Encyclopedias and dictionaries are usually not included in the bibliography.

16. BIBLICAL REFERENCE

16. Matt. 20.4-9 Revised Standard Version.

The Bible is usually not included in the bibliography.

Articles in periodicals

17. ARTICLE IN A JOURNAL PAGINATED BY VOLUME

17. Paula Findlen, "Possessing the Past: The Material World of the Italian Renaissance," <u>American Historical Review</u> 103 (1998): 86.

Findlen, Paula. "Possessing the Past: The Material World of the Italian Renaissance." <u>American Historical Review</u> 103 (1998): 83-114.

18. ARTICLE IN A JOURNAL PAGINATED BY ISSUE

18. Robert Darnton, "The Pursuit of Happiness," <u>Wilson Quarterly</u> 19, no. 4 (1995): 42.

Darnton, Robert. "The Pursuit of Happiness." <u>Wilson Quarterly</u> 19, no. 4 (1995): 42-52.

19. ARTICLE IN A MAGAZINE

19. Andrew Weil, "The New Politics of Coca," <u>New Yorker</u>, 15 May 1995, 70.

Weil, Andrew. "The New Politics of Coca." New
    Yorker, 15 May 1995, 70.

20. ARTICLE IN A NEWSPAPER

20. Lena H. Sun, "Chinese Feel the Strain of
a New Society," Washington Post, 13 June 1993,
sec. A.

Sun, Lena H. "Chinese Feel the Strain of a New
    Society." Washington Post, 13 June 1993, sec.
    A.

21. UNSIGNED ARTICLE

21. Radiation in Russia," U.S. News and World
Report, 9 August 1993, 41.

"Radiation in Russia." U.S. News and World
    Report, 9 August 1993, 40-42.

22. BOOK REVIEW

22. Dauril Alden, review of Vanguard of
Empire: Ships of Exploration in the Age of Colum-
bus, by Roger C. Smith, Journal of World History
6 (1995): 137.

Alden, Dauril. Review of Vanguard of Empire:
    Ships of Exploration in the Age of Columbus,
    by Roger C. Smith. Journal of World History
    6 (1995): 137-39.

Electronic sources

Although *The Chicago Manual of Style,* 14th ed., does not
include guidelines for documenting online sources, the
University of Chicago Press recommends following the
system developed by Andrew Harnack and Eugene
Kleppinger in *Online! A Reference Guide to Using Internet Sources,* 3rd ed. (Boston: Bedford/St. Martin's, 2000).
The examples of online sources given in this section are
based on Harnack and Kleppinger's guidelines; updates
can be found at <http://www.bedfordstmartins.com/
online>.

23. WORLD WIDE WEB SITE

    23. Yale Richmond and Duane Goehner, "Russian
Orthodoxy," Russian/American Contrasts, 3 December
1997, <http://www.goehner.com/russinfo.htm>
(15 March 1998).

Richmond, Yale, and Duane Goehner. "Russian Ortho-
        doxy." Russian/American Contrasts. 3 December
        1997. <http://www.goehner.com/russinfo.htm>
        (15 March 1998).

24. E-MAIL MESSAGE

    24. Eleanor Reeves, <elv92@uchic.edu> "Cold
War," 20 March 1998, personal e-mail (20 March
1998).

Reeves, Eleanor. <elv92@uchic.edu> "Cold War." 20
        March 1998. Personal e-mail (20 March 1998).

25. LISTSERV MESSAGE

    25. Nancy Stegall, <stegall@primenet.com>
"Web Publishing and Censorship," 2 February 1997,
<acw-1@ttacs6.ttu.edu> via <http://www.ttu.edu/
lists/acw-1> (18 March 1997).

Stegall, Nancy. <stegall@primenet.com> "Web
        Publishing and Censorship." 2 February 1997.
        <acw-1@ttacs6.ttu.edu> via <http://www.ttu.edu/
        lists/acw-1> (18 March 1997).

26. NEWSGROUP MESSAGE

    26. Richard J. Kennedy, <rkennedy@orednet.org>
"Re: Shakespeare's Daughters," 18 March 1997,
<humanities.lit.authors.shakespeare> (23 March
1997).

Kennedy, Richard J. <rkennedy@orednet.org> "Re:
        Shakespeare's Daughters." 18 March 1997.
        <humanities.lit.authors.shakespeare> (23
        March 1997).

27. SYNCHRONOUS COMMUNICATION

27. Diversity University MOO, 16 March 1997, group discussion, telnet moo.du.org (16 March 1997).

Diversity University MOO. 16 March 1997. Group discussion. Telnet moo.du.org (16 March 1997).

28. ELECTRONIC DATABASE

28. Paul D. Hightower, "Censorship," in Contemporary Education (Terre Haute: Indiana State University, School of Education, winter 1995), 66, Dialog, ERIC, ED 509251.

Hightower, Paul D. "Censorship." In Contemporary Education. Terre Haute: Indiana State University, School of Education, winter 1995. 66, Dialog, ERIC, ED 509251.

Other sources

29. GOVERNMENT DOCUMENT

29. U.S. Department of State, Foreign Relations of the United States: Diplomatic Papers, 1943 (Washington, D.C.: GPO, 1965), 562.

U.S. Department of State. Foreign Relations of the United States: Diplomatic Papers, 1943. Washington, D.C.: GPO, 1965.

30. UNPUBLISHED DISSERTATION

30. Cheryl D. Hoover, "East Germany's Revolution" (Ph.D. diss., Ohio State University, 1994), 450-51.

Hoover, Cheryl D. "East Germany's Revolution." Ph.D. diss., Ohio State University, 1994.

31. PERSONAL COMMUNICATION

31. Sara Lehman, letter to author, 13 August 1996.

Personal communications are not included in the bibliography.

32. INTERVIEW

32. Jesse Jackson, interview by Marshall Frady, Frontline, Public Broadcasting System, 30 April 1996.

Jackson, Jesse. Interview by Marshall Frady. Frontline. Public Broadcasting System, 30 April 1996.

33. FILM OR VIDEOTAPE

33. North by Northwest, prod. and dir. Alfred Hitchcock, 2 hr. 17 min., MGM/UA, 1959, videocassette.

North by Northwest. Produced and directed by Alfred Hitchcock. 2 hr. 17 min. MGM/UA, 1959. Videocassette.

34. SOUND RECORDING

34. Gustav Holst, The Planets, Royal Philharmonic, André Previn, Telarc compact disc 80133.

Holst, Gustav. The Planets. Royal Philharmonic. André Previn. Telarc compact disc 80133.

35. SOURCE QUOTED IN ANOTHER SOURCE

35. George Harmon Knoles, The Jazz Age Revisited: British Criticism of American Civilization during the 1920s (Stanford: Stanford University Press, 1955), 31, quoted in C. Vann Woodward, The Old World's New World (Oxford: Oxford University Press, 1991), 46.

Knoles, George Harmon. The Jazz Age Revisited: British Criticism of American Civilization during the 1920s, 31. Stanford: Stanford University Press, 1955. Quoted in C. Vann Woodward, The Old World's New World (Oxford: Oxford University Press, 1991), 46.

42   *Chicago* manuscript format

The following guidelines on manuscript formatting are based on *The Chicago Manual of Style,* 14th ed.

Preparing the paper

Title and identification.   On the title page, include the full title of your paper and your name. Your instructor may also want you to include the course title, the instructor's name, and the date. Do not type a number on the title page but count it in the manuscript; that is, the first page of text will usually be numbered page 2. See page 191 for a sample title page.

Margins and spacing.   Leave margins of at least one inch at the top, bottom, and sides of the page. Double-space the entire manuscript, including block quotations, but single-space individual entries in notes and the bibliography.

Pagination.   Using arabic numerals, number all pages except the title page in the upper right corner. Depending on your instructor's preference, you may also use a short title or your last name before page numbers to help identify pages in case they come loose from your manuscript. (See p. 192 for a sample *Chicago*-style manuscript page.)

Preparing the endnotes page

On page 193 are sample endnotes for a paper in *Chicago* style. (You may choose to or be required to use footnotes instead.) Endnote pages should be numbered consecutively with the rest of the manuscript, and the title "Notes" (without quotation marks) should be centered on the first page about one inch from the top of the page. Indent only the first line of each entry one-half inch (or five spaces) and begin the note with the arabic numeral corresponding to the number in the text. Follow the number with a period and one space. Do not indent any other lines of the entry. Single-space individual notes but double-space between notes.

Preparing the bibliography page

Typically, the notes in *Chicago*-style papers are followed by a bibliography, an alphabetically arranged list of all the works cited or consulted. Page 194 shows a sample bibliography in *Chicago* style.

Type the title "Bibliography" (without quotation marks), centered, about one inch from the top of the page. Number bibliography pages consecutively with the rest of the paper. Begin each entry at the left margin, and indent any additional lines one-half inch (or five spaces). Single-space individual entries but double-space between entries.

Alphabetize the bibliography by the last names of the authors (or editors); when a work has no author or editor, alphabetize by the first word of the title other than *A, An,* or *The.*

If your list includes two or more works by the same author, use three dashes (or three hyphens) instead of the author's name in all entries after the first. You may arrange the entries alphabetically by title or chronologically; be consistent throughout the bibliography.

The Massacre at Fort Pillow:
Holding Nathan Bedford Forrest Accountable

Ned Bishop

History 214
Professor Citro
22 March 1999

Although Northern newspapers of the time
no doubt exaggerated some of the Confederate
atrocities at Fort Pillow, most modern sources
agree that a massacre of Union troops took place
there on 12 April 1864. It seems clear that
Union soldiers, particularly black soldiers, were
killed after they had stopped fighting or had
surrendered or were being held prisoner. Less
clear is the role played by Confederate Major
General Nathan Bedford Forrest in leading his
troops. Although we will never know whether
Forrest directly ordered the massacre, evidence
suggests that he was responsible for it.

What happened at Fort Pillow?

Fort Pillow, Tennessee, which sat on a bluff
overlooking the Mississippi River, had been held
by the Union for two years. It was garrisoned by
580 men, 292 of them from the Sixth United States
Colored Heavy and Light Cavalry, 285 from the
white Thirteenth Tennessee Cavalry. Nathan Bedford
Forrest's troops numbered about 1,500 men.[1]

The Confederates attacked Fort Pillow on
12 April 1864, and had virtually surrounded the
fort by the time Forrest arrived on the battlefield. At 3:30 P.M., Forrest displayed a flag
of truce and sent in a demand for unconditional
surrender of the sort he had used before: "The
conduct of the officers and men garrisoning Fort
Pillow has been such as to entitle them to being
treated as prisoners of war. . . . Should my
demand be refused, I cannot be responsible for
the fate of your command."[2] Union Major William
Bradford, who had replaced Major Booth, killed
earlier by sharpshooters, asked for an hour to
consult.

Notes

1. John Cimprich and Robert C. Mainfort Jr., "Fort Pillow Revisited: New Evidence about an Old Controversy," Civil War History 28 (1982): 293-94.

2. Brian Steel Wills, A Battle from the Start: The Life of Nathan Bedford Forrest (New York: HarperCollins, 1992), 182.

3. Shelby Foote, The Civil War, a Narrative: Red River to Appomattox (New York: Vintage, 1986), 110.

4. Nathan Bedford Forrest, Report of Maj. Gen. Nathan Bedford Forrest, C. S. Army, Commanding Cavalry Battle of Fort Pillow, 26 April 1864, <http://www.civilwarhome.com/forrest.htm> (23 April 1999), 2.

5. Jack Hurst, Nathan Bedford Forrest: A Biography (New York: Knopf, 1993), 174.

6. Foote, 111.

7. Cimprich and Mainfort, 305.

8. Cimprich and Mainfort, 299.

9. Foote, 110.

10. Wills, 187.

11. Albert Castel, "The Fort Pillow Massacre: A Fresh Examination of the Evidence," Civil War History 4 (1958): 44-45.

12. Cimprich and Mainfort, 300.

13. Hurst, 177.

14. Hurst, 177.

15. Dudley Taylor Cornish, The Sable Arm: Black Troops in the Union Army, 1861-1865 (Lawrence, Kans.: University Press of Kansas, 1987), 175.

16. Foote, 111.

17. Cimprich and Mainfort, 304.

Bibliography

Castel, Albert. "The Fort Pillow Massacre: A
    Fresh Examination of the Evidence." Civil War
    History 4 (1958): 37-50.

Cimprich, John, and Robert C. Mainfort Jr. "Fort
    Pillow Revisited: New Evidence about an Old
    Controversy," Civil War History 28 (1982):
    293-306.

Cornish, Dudley Taylor. The Sable Arm: Black
    Troops in the Union Army, 1861-1865.
    Lawrence, Kans.: University Press of Kansas,
    1987.

Foote, Shelby. The Civil War, a Narrative: Red
    River to Appomattox. New York: Vintage, 1986.

Forrest, Nathan Bedford. Report of Maj. Gen.
    Nathan Bedford Forrest, C. S. Army,
    Commanding Cavalry Battle of Fort Pillow. 26
    April 1864. <http://www.civilwarhome.com/
    forrest.htm> (23 April 1999).

Hurst, Jack. Nathan Bedford Forrest: A Biography.
    New York: Knopf, 1993.

McPherson, James M. Battle Cry of Freedom: The
    Civil War Era. New York, Oxford University
    Press, 1988.

Wills, Brian Steel. A Battle from the Start: The
    Life of Nathan Bedford Forrest. New York:
    HarperCollins, 1992.

G
L
O
S
S
A
R
I
E
S

Glossary of Usage
Glossary of Grammatical Terms

This glossary includes words commonly confused, words commonly misused, and words that are nonstandard. It also lists colloquialisms that may be appropriate in informal speech but are often considered inappropriate in formal writing.

a, an Use *an* before a vowel sound, *a* before a consonant sound: *an apple, a peach.* Problems sometimes arise with words beginning with *h*. If the *h* is silent, the word begins with a vowel sound, so use *an: an hour, an heir, an honest senator, an honorable deed.* If the *h* is pronounced, the word begins with a consonant sound, so use *a: a hospital, a hymn, a historian, a hotel.* When an abbreviation or acronym begins with a vowel sound, use *an: an EKG, an MRI, an AIDS patient.*

accept, except *Accept* is a verb meaning "to receive." *Except* is usually a preposition meaning "excluding." *I will accept all the packages except that one. Except* is also a verb meaning "to exclude." *Please except that item from the list.*

adapt, adopt *Adapt* means "to adjust or become accustomed"; it is usually followed by *to. Adopt* means "to take as one's own." *Our family adopted a Vietnamese orphan, who quickly adapted to his new surroundings.*

adverse, averse *Adverse* means "unfavorable." *Averse* means "opposed" or "reluctant"; it is usually followed by *to. I am averse to your proposal because it could have an adverse impact on the economy.*

advice, advise *Advice* is a noun, *advise* a verb. *We advise you to follow John's advice.*

affect, effect *Affect* is usually a verb meaning "to influence." *Effect* is usually a noun meaning "result." *The drug did not affect the disease, and it had several adverse side effects. Effect* can also be a verb meaning "to bring about." *Only the president can effect such a dramatic change.*

all ready, already *All ready* means "completely prepared." *Already* means "previously." *Susan was all ready for the concert, but her friends had already left.*

all right *All right* is always written as two words. *Alright* is nonstandard.

all together, altogether *All together* means "everyone gathered." *Altogether* means "entirely." *We were not al-*

together certain that we could bring the family all *together* for the reunion.

allusion, illusion An *allusion* is an indirect reference; an *illusion* is a misconception or false impression. *Did you catch my allusion to Shakespeare? Mirrors give the room an illusion of depth.*

a lot *A lot* is two words. Do not write *alot.*

among, between Ordinarily, use *among* with three or more entities, *between* with two. *The prize was divided among several contestants. You have a choice between carrots and beans.*

amount, number Use *amount* with quantities that cannot be counted; use *number* with those that can. *This recipe calls for a large amount of sugar. We have a large number of toads in our garden.*

an See *a, an.*

and/or Avoid *and/or* except in technical or legal documents.

anxious *Anxious* means "worried" or "apprehensive." In formal writing, avoid using *anxious* to mean "eager." *We are eager* [not *anxious*] *to see your new house.*

anybody, anyone See pages 22–23 and 33.

anyone, any one *Anyone,* an indefinite pronoun, means "any person at all." *Any one* refers to a particular person or thing in a group. *Anyone from Chicago may choose any one of the games on display.*

anyways, anywheres *Anyways* and *anywheres* are nonstandard for *anyway* and *anywhere.*

as *As* is sometimes used to mean "because." But do not use it if there is any chance of ambiguity. *We canceled the picnic because* [not *as*] *it began raining.* An *as* here could mean "because" or "when."

as, like See *like, as.*

awful The adjective *awful* means "awe-inspiring." Colloquially it is used to mean "terrible" or "bad." The adverb *awfully* is sometimes used in conversation as an intensifier meaning "very." In formal writing, avoid these colloquial uses. *I was very* [not *awfully*] *upset last night.*

awhile, a while *Awhile* is an adverb; it can modify a verb, but it cannot be the object of a preposition such as *for.* The two-word form *a while* is a noun preceded by an article and therefore can be the object of a preposition. *Stay awhile. Stay for a while.*

back up, backup   *Back up* is a verb phrase. *Back up the car carefully. Be sure to back up your hard drive.* A *backup* is a duplicate of electronically stored data. *Keep your backup in a safe place. Backup* can also be used as an adjective. *I regularly create backup disks.*

bad, badly   *Bad* is an adjective, *badly* an adverb. *They felt bad about being early and ruining the surprise. Her arm hurt badly after she slid into second.* (See section 13.)

being as, being that   *Being as* and *being that* are nonstandard expressions. Write *because* or *since* instead.

beside, besides   *Beside* is a preposition meaning "at the side of" or "next to." *Annie Oakley slept with her gun beside her bed. Besides* is a preposition meaning "except" or "in addition to." *No one besides Terrie can have that ice cream. Besides* is also an adverb meaning "in addition." *I'm not hungry; besides, I don't like ice cream.*

between   See *among, between.*

bring, take   Use *bring* when an object is being transported toward you, *take* when it is being moved away. *Please bring me a glass of water. Please take these magazines to Mr. Scott.*

burst, bursted; bust, busted   *Burst* is an irregular verb meaning "to come open or fly apart suddenly or violently." The past-tense form *bursted* is nonstandard. *Bust* and *busted* are slang for *burst* and, along with *bursted,* should not be used in formal writing.

can, may   *Can* is traditionally reserved for ability, *may* for permission. *Can you ski down the advanced slope without falling? May I help you?*

capital, capitol   *Capital* refers to a city, *capitol* to a building where lawmakers meet. *The residents of the state capital protested the development plans. The capitol has undergone extensive renovations. Capital* also refers to wealth or resources.

cite, site   *Cite* means "to quote as an authority or example." *Site* is usually a noun meaning "a particular place." *He cited the zoning law in his argument against the proposed site of the gas station.* Locations on the Internet are usually referred to as *sites. The library's Web site improves every week.*

coarse, course   *Coarse* means "crude" or "rough in texture." *The coarse weave of the wall hanging gave it a three-dimensional quality. Course* usually refers to a path, a playing field, or a unit of study; the expression *of course* means "certainly." *I plan to take a course in car repair this summer. Of course, you are welcome to join me.*

complement, compliment   *Complement* is a verb meaning "to go with or complete" or a noun meaning "something that completes." *Compliment* as a verb means "to flatter"; as a noun it means "flattering remark." *Her skill at rushing the net complements his skill at volleying. Sheiying's music arrangements receive many compliments.*

conscience, conscious   *Conscience* is a noun meaning "moral principles"; *conscious* is an adjective meaning "aware or alert." *Let your conscience be your guide. Were you conscious of his love for you?*

continual, continuous   *Continual* means "repeated regularly and frequently." *She grew weary of the continual telephone calls. Continuous* means "extended or prolonged without out interruption." *The broken siren made a continuous wail.*

could care less   *Could care less* is a nonstandard expression. Write *couldn't care less* instead.

could of   *Could of* is nonstandard for *could have.*

council, counsel   A *council* is a deliberative body, and a *councilor* is a member of such a body. *Counsel* usually means "advice" and can also mean "lawyer"; *counselor* is one who gives advice or guidance. *The councilors met to draft the council's position paper. The pastor offered wise counsel to the troubled teenager.*

criteria   *Criteria* is the plural of *criterion,* which means "a standard, rule, or test on which a judgment or decision can be based." *The only criterion for the job is a willingness to work overtime.*

data   *Data* is a plural noun technically meaning "facts or propositions." But *data* is increasingly being accepted as a singular noun. *The new data suggest* [or *suggests*] *that our theory is correct.* (The singular datum is rarely used.)

different from, different than   Ordinarily, write *different from. Your sense of style is different from Jim's.* However, *different than* is acceptable to avoid an awkward construction. *Please let me know if your plans are different than* [to avoid *from what*] *they were six weeks ago.*

don't   *Don't* is the contraction for *do not. I don't want any. Don't* should not be used as the contraction for *does not,* which is *doesn't. He doesn't* [not *don't*] *want any.*

due to *Due to* is an adjective phrase and should not be used as a preposition meaning "because of." *The trip was canceled because of* [not *due to*] *lack of interest. Due to* is acceptable as a subject complement and usually follows a form of the verb *be. His success was due to hard work.*

each See pages 22–23 and 33.

effect See *affect, effect.*

e.g. Use *for example* or *for instance* in formal writing.

either See pages 22–23 and 33.

enthused As an adjective, *enthusiastic* is preferred. *The children were enthusiastic* [not *enthused*] *about going to the circus.*

etc. Avoid ending a list with *etc.* It is more emphatic to end with an example, and in most contexts readers will understand that the list is not exhaustive. When you don't wish to end with an example, *and so on* is more graceful than *etc.*

everybody, everyone See pages 22–23 and 33.

everyone, every one *Everyone* is an indefinite pronoun. *Everyone wanted to go. Every one,* the pronoun *one* preceded by the adjective *every,* means "each individual or thing in a particular group." *Every one* is usually followed by *of. Every one of the missing books was found.*

except See *accept, except.*

farther, further *Farther* describes distances. *Detroit is farther from Miami than I thought. Further* suggests quantity or degree. *You extended the curfew further than you should have.*

fewer, less *Fewer* refers to items that can be counted; *less* refers to general amounts. *Fewer people are living in the city. Please put less sugar in my tea.*

firstly *Firstly* sounds pretentious, and it leads to the ungainly series *firstly, secondly, thirdly, fourthly,* and so on. Write *first, second, third* instead.

further See *farther, further.*

good, well *Good* is an adjective, *well* an adverb. *He hasn't felt good about his game since he sprained his wrist last season. She performed well on the uneven parallel bars.* (See section 13.)

hanged, hung *Hanged* is the past-tense and past-participle form of the verb *hang,* meaning "to execute." *The prisoner was hanged at dawn. Hung* is the past-tense and past-participle form of the verb *hang,* meaning "to fasten or suspend." *The stockings were hung by the chimney with care.*

hardly Avoid expressions such as *can't hardly* and *not hardly,* which are considered double negatives. *I can* [not *can't*] *hardly describe my elation at getting the job.*

he At one time *he* was used to mean "he or she." Today such usage is inappropriate. See pages 18 and 33 for alternative constructions.

hisself *Hisself* is nonstandard. Use *himself.*

hopefully Some usage experts object to the use of *hopefully* as a sentence adverb, apparently on grounds of clarity. To be on the safe side, avoid using *hopefully* in sentences such as the following: *Hopefully, your son will recover soon.* At least some educated readers will want you to indicate who is doing the hoping. *I hope that your son will recover soon.*

hung See *hanged, hung.*

i.e. Use *that is* in formal writing.

illusion See *allusion, illusion.*

impact *Impact* is commonly used as a noun. Avoid using the expression *impact on* as a verb. *The legislation had an impact on* [not *impacted on*] *our company's policies.*

imply, infer *Imply* means "to suggest or state indirectly"; *infer* means "to draw a conclusion." *John implied that he knew all about computers, but the interviewer inferred that John was inexperienced.*

in regards to *In regards to* confuses two different phrases: *in regard to* and *as regards.* Use one or the other. *In regard to* [or *As regards*] *the contract, ignore the first clause.*

irregardless *Irregardless* is nonstandard. Use *regardless.*

is when, is where These mixed constructions are often incorrectly used in definitions. *A run-off election is a second election held to break a tie* [not *is when a second election is held to break a tie*].

it is *It is* is nonstandard when used to mean "there is." *There is* [not *It is*] *a fly in my soup.*

its, it's *Its* is a possessive pronoun; *it's* is a contraction for *it is. The dog licked its wound whenever its owner walked into the room. It's a perfect day to walk the twenty-mile trail.*

kind of, sort of Avoid using *kind of* or *sort of* to mean "somewhat." *The movie was a little* [not *kind of*] *boring.* Do not put *a* after either phrase. *That kind of* [not *kind of a*] *salesclerk annoys me.*

lead, led *Lead* is a noun referring to a metal. *Led* is the past tense of the verb *to lead. He led me to the treasure.*

learn, teach *Learn* means "to gain knowledge"; *teach* means "to impart knowledge." *I must teach* [not *learn*] *my sister to read.*

leave, let Avoid the nonstandard use of *leave* ("to exit") to mean *let* ("to permit"). *Let* [not *Leave*] *me help you with the dishes.*

less See *fewer, less.*

let, leave See *leave, let.*

liable *Liable* means "obligated" or "responsible." Do not use it to mean "likely." *You're likely* [not *liable*] *to trip if you don't tie your shoelaces.*

lie, lay *Lie* is an intransitive verb meaning "to recline or rest on a surface." Its forms are *lie, lay, lain, lying,* and *lies. Lay* is a transitive verb meaning "to put or place." Its forms are *lay, laid, laid, laying,* and *lays.* (See pp. 26–27.)

like, as *Like* is a preposition, not a subordinating conjunction. It should be followed only by a noun or a noun phrase. *As* is a subordinating conjunction that introduces a subordinate clause. In casual speech you may say *She looks like she hasn't slept* or *You don't know her like I do.* But in formal writing, use *as. She looks as if she hasn't slept. You don't know her as I do.*

loose, lose *Loose* is an adjective meaning "not securely fastened." *Lose* is a verb meaning "to misplace" or "to not win." *Did you lose your only loose pair of work pants?*

may See *can, may.*

maybe, may be *Maybe* is an adverb meaning "possibly"; *may be* is a verb phrase. *Maybe the sun will shine tomorrow. Tomorrow may be a brighter day.*

may of, might of *May of* and *might of* are nonstandard for *may have* and *might have.*

media, medium *Media* is the plural of *medium. Of all the media that cover the Olympics, television is the medium that best captures the spectacle of the events.*

most Avoid *most* to mean "almost." *Almost* [not *Most*] *everyone went to the parade.*

must of See *may of.*

myself *Myself* is a reflexive or intensive pronoun. Reflexive: *I cut myself.* Intensive: *I will drive you myself.* Do not use *myself* in place of *I* or *me*: *He gave the plants to Melinda and me* [not *myself*].

neither See pages 22–23 and 33.

none See pages 22–23 and 33.

nowheres *Nowheres* is nonstandard for *nowhere.*

number See *amount, number.*

of Use the verb *have,* not the preposition *of,* after the verbs *could, should, would, may, might,* and *must. They must have* [not *must of*] *left early.*

off of *Off* is sufficient. Omit *of.*

passed, past *Passed* is the past tense of the verb *to pass. Emily passed me another slice of cake. Past* usually means "belonging to a former time" or "beyond a time or place." *Our past president spoke until past midnight. The hotel is just past the next intersection.*

plus *Plus* should not be used to join independent clauses. *This raincoat is dirty; moreover* [not *plus*], *it has a hole in it.*

precede, proceed *Precede* means "to come before." *Proceed* means "to go forward." *As we proceeded up the mountain, we noticed fresh tracks in the mud, evidence that a group of hikers had preceded us.*

principal, principle *Principal* is a noun meaning "the head of a school or organization" or "a sum of money." It is also an adjective meaning "most important." *Principle* is a noun meaning "a basic truth or law." *The principal expelled her for three principal reasons. We believe in the principle of equal justice for all.*

proceed, precede See *precede, proceed.*

quote, quotation *Quote* is a verb; *quotation* is a noun. Avoid using *quote* as a shortened form of the noun. *Her quotations* [not *quotes*] *from the* Upanishads *intrigued us.*

real, really *Real* is an adjective; *really* is an adverb. *Real* is sometimes used informally as an adverb, but avoid this use in formal writing. *She was really* [not *real*] *angry.* (See section 13.)

reason is because Use *that* instead of *because. The reason I'm late is that* [not *because*] *my car broke down.*

reason why The expression *reason why* is redundant. *The reason* [not *The reason why*] *Jones lost the election is clear.*

respectfully, respectively   *Respectfully* means "showing or marked by respect." *He respectfully submitted his opinion to the judge. Respectively* means "each in the order given." *John, Tom, and Larry were a butcher, a baker, and a lawyer, respectively.*

sensual, sensuous   *Sensual* means "gratifying the physical senses," especially those associated with sexual pleasure. *Sensuous* means "pleasing to the senses," especially those involved in the experience of art, music, and nature. *The sensuous music and balmy air led the dancers to more sensual movements.*

set, sit   *Set* means "to put" or "to place"; *sit* means "to be seated." *She set the dough in a warm corner of the kitchen. The cat sits in the warmest part of the room.*

should of   *Should of* is nonstandard for *should have.*

since   Do not use *since* to mean "because" if there is any chance of ambiguity. *Because* [not *Since*] *we won the game, we have been celebrating with a pitcher of beer. Since* here could mean "because" or "from the time that."

sit   See *set, sit.*

site, cite   See *cite, site.*

somebody, someone, something   See pages 22–23 and 33.

suppose to   Write *supposed to.*

sure and   *Sure and* is nonstandard for *sure to. Be sure to* [not *sure and*] *bring a gift to the host.*

take   See *bring, take.*

than, then   *Than* is a conjunction used in comparisons; *then* is an adverb denoting time. *That pizza is more than I can eat. Tom laughed, and then we recognized him.*

that   See *who, which, that.*

that, which   Many writers reserve *that* for restrictive clauses, *which* for nonrestrictive clauses. (See p. 60.)

theirselves   *Theirselves* is nonstandard for *themselves.*

them   The use of *them* in place of *those* is nonstandard. *Please send those* [not *them*] *letters to the sponsors.*

there, their, they're   *There* is an adverb specifying place; it is also an expletive. Adverb: *Sylvia is lying there unconscious.* Expletive: *There are two plums left. Their* is a possessive pronoun. *Fred and Jane finally washed their car. They're* is a contraction of *they are. Surprisingly, they're late today.*

they The use of *they* to indicate possession is nonstandard. Use *their* instead. *Cindy and Sam decided to sell their* [not *they*] *boat.*

to, too, two *To* is a preposition; *too* is an adverb; *two* is a number. *Too many of your shots slice to the left, but the last two were right on the mark.*

toward, towards *Toward* and *towards* are generally interchangeable, although *toward* is preferred.

try and *Try and* is nonstandard for *try to. I will try to* [not *try and*] *be better about writing to you.*

unique Avoid expressions such as *most unique, more straight, less perfect, very round.* It is illogical to suggest degrees of such absolute concepts as *unique.*

use to, suppose to *Use to* and *suppose to* are nonstandard for *used to* and *supposed to.*

utilize *Utilize* means "to make use of." It often sounds pretentious; in most cases, *use* is sufficient. *I used* (not *utilized*) *the best workers to get the job done fast.*

wait for, wait on *Wait for* means "to be in readiness for" or "await." *Wait on* means "to serve." *We're waiting for* [not *waiting on*] *Ruth before we can leave.*

ways *Ways* is colloquial when used in place of *way* to mean "distance." *The city is a long way* [not *ways*] *from here.*

weather, whether The noun *weather* refers to the state of the atmosphere. *Whether* is a conjunction referring to a choice between alternatives. *We wondered whether the weather would clear up in time for our picnic.*

well, good See *good, well.*

where Do not use *where* in place of *that. I heard that* [not *where*] *the crime rate is increasing.*

which See *that, which* and *who, which, that.*

while Avoid using *while* to mean "although" or "whereas" if there is any chance of ambiguity. *Although* [not *While*] *Gloria lost money in the slot machine, Tom won it at roulette.* Here *While* could mean either "although" or "at the same time that."

who, which, that Use *who,* not *which,* to refer to persons. Generally, use *that* to refer to things or, occasionally, to a group or class of people. *Fans wondered how an old man who* [not *that* or *which*] *walked with a limp could play football. The team that scores the most points in this game will win the tournament.*

who, whom *Who* is used for subjects and subject complements; *whom* is used for objects. (See pp. 39–40.)

who's, whose *Who's* is a contraction of *who is; whose* is a possessive pronoun. *Who's ready for more popcorn? Whose coat is this?*

would of *Would of* is nonstandard for *would have.*

you In formal writing, avoid *you* in an indefinite sense meaning "anyone." *Any spectator* [not *You*] *could tell by the way John caught the ball that his throw would be too late.* (See pp. 35–36.)

your, you're *Your* is a possessive pronoun; *you're* is a contraction of *you are. Is that your new motorcycle? You're on the list of finalists.*

44 Glossary of grammatical terms

This glossary gives definitions for parts of speech, such as nouns; parts of sentences, such as subjects; and types of sentences, clauses, and phrases.

If you are looking up the name of an error (sentence fragment, for example), consult the index or the table of contents instead.

absolute phrase A word group that modifies a whole clause or sentence, usually consisting of a noun followed by a participle or participial phrase. *His tone suggesting no hint of humor,* the minister told us to love our enemies because it would drive them nuts.

active vs. passive voice When a verb is in the active voice, the subject of the sentence does the action. The early *bird catches* the early worm. In the passive voice, the subject receives the action: The early *worm is* sometimes *caught* by the early bird. Often the actor does not appear in the passive-voice sentence: The early *worm is* sometimes *caught.* (See also pp. 3–5 and 32.)

adjective A word used to modify (describe) a noun or pronoun: the *lame* dog, *rare old* stamps, *sixteen* candles. Adjectives usually answer one of these questions: Which one? What kind of? How many or how much? (See also pp. 40–42.)

adjective clause A subordinate clause that modifies a noun or pronoun. An adjective clause begins with a relative pronoun (*who, whom, whose, which, that*) or a relative adverb (*when, where*) and usually appears right after the word it modifies: The arrow *that has left the bow* never returns.

adverb   A word used to modify a verb, an adjective, or another adverb: rides *smoothly, unusually* attractive, *very* slowly. An adverb usually answers one of these questions: When? Where? How? Why? Under what conditions? To what degree? (See also pp. 10–12.)

adverb clause   A subordinate clause that modifies a verb (or occasionally an adjective or adverb). An adverb clause begins with a subordinating conjunction such as *although, because, if, unless,* or *when* and usually appears at the beginning or the end of a sentence: *When the well is dry,* we know the worth of water. Don't talk *unless you can improve the silence.*

agreement   See pages 21–25 and 32–34.

antecedent   A noun or pronoun to which a pronoun refers: When the *wheel* squeaks, *it* is greased. *Wheel* is the antecedent of the pronoun *it.*

appositive   A noun or noun phrase that renames a nearby noun or pronoun: Politicians, *acrobats at heart,* can lean on both sides of an issue at once.

article   The word *a, an, the,* used to mark a noun. (See also pp. 48–51.)

case   See pages 36–40.

clause   A word group containing a subject, a verb, and any objects, complements, or modifiers of the verb. See *independent clause, subordinate clause.*

complement   See *subject complement, object complement.*

complex sentence   A sentence consisting of one independent clause and one or more subordinate clauses. In the following example, the subordinate clause is italicized: Do not insult the mother alligator *until you have crossed the river.*

compound-complex sentence   A sentence consisting of at least two independent clauses and at least one subordinate clause. In the following example, the subordinate clauses are italicized: Tell me *what you eat,* and I will tell you *what you are.*

compound sentence   A sentence consisting of two independent clauses. The clauses are usually joined by a comma and a coordinating conjunction (*and, but, or, nor, for, so, yet*) or by a semicolon: One arrow is easily broken, but you can't

break a bundle of ten. Love is blind; envy has its eyes wide
open.

conjunction   A joining word. See *coordinating conjunction,
correlative conjunction, subordinating conjunction, conjunctive adverb.*

conjunctive adverb   An adverb used with a semicolon to
connect independent clauses: If an animal does something,
we call it instinct; *however,* if we do the same thing, we call
it intelligence. The most commonly used conjunctive adverbs are *consequently, furthermore, however, moreover, nevertheless, then, therefore,* and *thus.* See page 65 for a more
complete list.

coordinating conjunction   One of the following words,
used to join elements of equal grammatical rank: *and, but,
or, nor, for, so, yet.*

correlative conjunction   A pair of conjunctions connecting grammatically equal elements: *either . . . or, neither . . .
nor, whether . . . or, not only . . . but also,* and *both . . . and.*

count nouns   See page 48.

demonstrative pronoun   A pronoun used to identify or
point to a noun: *this, that, these, those. This* hanging will
surely be a lesson to me.

direct object   A word or word group that receives the action of the verb: The little snake studies *the ways of the big
serpent.* The complete direct object is *the ways of the big
serpent.* The simple direct object is always a noun or pronoun, such as *ways.*

expletive   The word *there* or *it* when used at the beginning of a sentence to delay the subject: *There* are many
paths to the top of the mountain. *It* is not good to wake a
sleeping lion. The delayed subjects are the noun *paths* and
the infinitive phrase *to wake a sleeping lion.*

gerund   A verb form ending in *-ing,* used as a noun:
Continual *dripping* wears away a stone. *Dripping* is used as
the subject of the verb *wears away.*

gerund phrase   A gerund and its objects, complements, or
modifiers. A gerund phrase always functions as a noun,
usually as a subject, a subject complement, or a direct object. In the following example, the phrase functions as a
subject: *Justifying a fault* doubles it.

helping verb   One of the following words, when used with
a main verb: *be, am, is, are, was, were, being, been; has, have,
had; do, does, did; can, will, shall, should, could, would, may,*

might, must. Helping verbs always precede main verbs: *will work, is working, had worked.*

indefinite pronoun A pronoun that refers to a nonspecific person or thing: *Anyone* who serves God for money will serve the Devil for better wages. The most common indefinite pronouns are *all, another, any, anybody, anyone, anything, both, each, either, everybody, everyone, everything, few, many, neither, nobody, none, no one, nothing, one, some, somebody, someone, something.*

independent clause A clause (containing a subject and a verb) that can or does stand alone as a sentence. Every sentence consists of at least one independent clause. In addition, many sentences contain subordinate clauses that function as adjectives, adverbs, or nouns. See also *subordinate clause.*

indirect object A noun or pronoun that names to whom or for whom the action is done: Fate gives *us* our relatives. An indirect object always precedes a direct object, in this case *our relatives.*

infinitive The word *to* followed by a verb: *to think, to dream.*

infinitive phrase An infinitive and its objects, complements, or modifiers. An infinitive phrase can function as a noun, an adjective, or an adverb: *To side with truth* is noble. We do not have the right *to abandon the poor.* Do not use a hatchet *to remove a fly from your friend's forehead.*

intensive or reflexive pronoun A pronoun ending in *-self: myself, yourself, himself, herself, itself, ourselves, yourselves, themselves.* An intensive pronoun emphasizes a noun or another pronoun: I *myself* don't understand my moods. A reflexive pronoun names a receiver of an action identical with the doer of the action: Did you cut *yourself*?

interjection A word expressing surprise or emotion: *Oh! Wow! Hey! Hooray!*

interrogative pronoun A pronoun used to open a question: *who, whom, whose, which, what. What* does history teach us?

intransitive verb See *transitive and intransitive verbs.*

irregular verb See *regular and irregular verbs.* Or see pages 25–29.

linking verb A verb that links a subject to a subject complement, a word or word group that renames or describes the subject: Prejudice *is* the child of ignorance. Good medicine sometimes *tastes* bitter. The most common linking verbs are forms of *be: be, am, is, are, was, were, being, been.* The following verbs sometimes function as linking verbs: *appear, become, feel, grow, look, make, seem, smell, sound, taste.*

modifier A word, phrase, or clause that describes or qualifies the meaning of a word. Modifiers include adjectives, adverbs, prepositional phrases, participial phrases, some infinitive phrases, and adjective and adverb clauses.

mood See pages 31–32.

noun The name of a person, place, or thing: The *cat* in *gloves* catches no *mice.* Nouns are classified for a variety of purposes. When capitalization is the issue, we speak of *proper* versus *common* nouns (see pp. 81–82). If the problem involves the use of articles, we distinguish between *count* nouns and *noncount* nouns (see p. 48). Most nouns come in *singular* and *plural* forms; *collective nouns* may be either singular or plural (see pp. 23, 34). *Possessive* nouns require an apostrophe (see pp. 69–70).

noun clause A subordinate clause that functions as a noun, usually as a subject, a subject complement, or a direct object. In the following sentence, the italicized noun clauses function as subject and subject complement: *What history teaches us* is *that we have never learned anything from it.* Noun clauses usually begin with *how, who, whom, that, what, whether,* or *why.*

noun equivalent A word or word group that functions like a noun: a pronoun, a noun and its modifiers, a gerund phrase, some infinitive phrases, a noun clause.

object See *direct object, indirect object.*

object complement A word or word group that renames or describes a direct object. It always appears after the direct object: Our fears do make us *traitors.* Love makes all hard hearts *gentle.*

object of a preposition See *prepositional phrase.*

participial phrase A present or past participle and its objects, complements, or modifiers. A participial phrase always functions as an adjective describing a noun or pronoun. Usually it appears before or after the word it modifies: *Being weak,* foxes are distinguished by superior tact. Truth *kept in the dark* will never save the world.

participle, past A verb form usually ending in *-d, -ed, -n, -en,* or *-t: asked, spoken, stolen.* Although past participles usually function as main verbs (was *asked,* had *spoken*), they may also be used as adjectives (the *stolen* car).

participle, present A verb form ending in *-ing.* Although present participles usually function as main verbs (is *rising*), they may also be used as adjectives (the *rising* tide).

parts of speech A system for classifying words. Many words can function as more than one part of speech. See *noun, pronoun, verb, adjective, adverb, preposition, conjunction, interjection.*

passive voice See *active vs. passive voice.*

personal pronoun One of the following pronouns, used to refer to a specific person or thing: *I, me, you, she, her, he, him, it, we, us, they, them.* Admonish your friends in private; praise *them* in public.

phrase A word group that lacks a subject, a verb, or both. Most phrases function within sentences as adjectives, as adverbs, or as nouns. See *absolute phrase, appositive, gerund phrase, infinitive phrase, participial phrase, prepositional phrase.*

possessive case See pages 69–70.

possessive pronoun A pronoun used to indicate ownership: *my, mine, your, yours, her, hers, his, its, our, ours, your, yours, their, theirs.* A cock has great influence on *his* own dunghill.

predicate A verb and any objects, complements, and modifiers that go with it: A clean glove *often hides a dirty hand.*

preposition A word placed before a noun or noun equivalent to form a phrase modifying another word in the sentence. The preposition indicates the relation between the noun (or noun equivalent) and the word the phrase modifies. The most common prepositions are *about, above, across, after, against, along, among, around, at, before, behind, below, beside, besides, between, beyond, by, down, during, except, for, from, in, inside, into, like, near, next, of, off, on, onto, out, outside, over, past, since, than, through, to, toward, under, unlike, until, up, with,* and *without.*

prepositional phrase A phrase beginning with a preposition and ending with a noun or noun equivalent (called the *object of the preposition*). Most prepositional phrases function as adjectives or adverbs. Adjective phrases usually come right after the noun or pronoun they modify: Variety is the spice *of life.* Adverb phrases usually appear at the beginning or the end of the sentence: *To the ant,* a few drops of rain are a flood. Do not judge a tree *by its bark.*

progressive verb forms   See page 30.

pronoun   A word used in place of a noun. Usually the pronoun substitutes for a specific noun, known as its antecedent. In the following example, *elephant* is the antecedent of the pronoun *him*: When an *elephant* is in trouble, even a frog will kick *him*. See also *demonstrative pronoun, indefinite pronoun, intensive or reflexive pronoun, interrogative pronoun, personal pronoun, possessive pronoun, relative pronoun.*

regular and irregular verbs   When a verb is regular, both the past tense and past participle are formed by adding *-ed* or *-d* to the base form of the word: *walk, walked, walked.* Irregular verbs are formed in a variety of other ways: *ride, rode, ridden; begin, began, begun; go, went, gone;* and so on. See also pages 25–29.

relative adverb   The word *when* or *where,* when used to introduce an adjective clause.

relative pronoun   One of the following words, when used to introduce an adjective clause: *who, whom, whose, which, that.* A fable is a bridge *that* leads to truth.

sentence   A word group consisting of at least one independent clause. See also *simple sentence, compound sentence, complex sentence, compound-complex sentence.*

simple sentence   A sentence consisting of one independent clause and no subordinate clauses: The frog in the well knows nothing of the ocean.

subject   A word or word group that names who or what the sentence is about. In the following example, the complete subject (the simple subject and all of its modifiers) is italicized: *Historical books that contain no lies* are tedious. The simple subject is *books.* See also *subject after verb, understood subject.*

subject after verb   Although the subject normally precedes the verb, sentences are sometimes inverted. In the following example, the subject *the real tinsel* comes after the verb *lies:* Behind the phony tinsel of Hollywood lies the real tinsel. When a sentence begins with the expletive *there* or *it,* the subject always follows the verb. See *expletive.*

subject complement   A word or word group that follows a linking verb and either renames or describes the subject of the sentence. If the subject complement renames the subject, it is a noun or a noun equivalent: The handwriting on the wall may be *a forgery.* If it describes the subject, it is an adjective: Love is *blind.*

subjunctive mood   See pages 31–32.

subordinate clause   A clause (containing a subject and verb) that cannot stand alone as a sentence. Subordinate clauses function within sentences as adjectives, adverbs, or nouns. They begin with subordinating conjuctions such as *although, because, if,* and *until* or with relative pronouns such as *who, which,* and *that.* See *adjective clause, adverb clause, noun clause.*

subordinating conjunction   A word that introduces a subordinate clause and indicates its relation to the rest of the sentence. The most common subordinating conjunctions are *after, although, as, as if, because, before, even though, if, since, so that, than, that, though, unless, until, when, where, whether,* and *while.* Note: The relative pronouns *who, whom, whose, which,* and *that* also introduce subordinate clauses.

tenses   See pages 29–31.

transitive and intransitive verbs   Transitive verbs take direct objects, nouns or noun equivalents that receive the action. In the following example, the transitive verb *loves* takes the direct object *its mother:* A spoiled child never *loves* its mother. Intransitive verbs do not take direct objects: Money *talks.* If any words follow an intransitive verb, they are adverbs or word groups functioning as adverbs: The sun *will set* without your assistance.

understood subject   The subject *you* when it is understood but not actually present in the sentence. Understood subjects occur in sentences that issue commands or advice: [*You*] Hitch your wagon to a star.

verb   A word that expresses action (*jump, think*) or being (*is, was*). A sentence's verb is composed of a main verb possibly preceded by one or more helping verbs: The best fish *swim* near the bottom. A marriage *is* not *built* in a day. Verbs have five forms: the base form, or dictionary form (*walk, ride*), the past-tense form (*walked, rode*), the past participle (*walked, ridden*), the present participle (*walking, riding*) and the *-s* form (*walks, rides*).

verbal phrase   See *gerund phrase, infinitive phrase, participial phrase.*

A List of Style Manuals

A useful list of sources (both print and online) and documentation models for many disciplines can be found on a Web site that accompanies this text: *Research and Documentation Online* <http://www.bedfordstmartins.com/hacker/ resdoc>.

A Pocket Style Manual describes three commonly used systems of documentation: MLA, used in English and the humanities (see section 31); APA, used in psychology and the social sciences (see section 36); and *Chicago*, used primarily in history (see section 41). Following is a list of style manuals used in a variety of disciplines.

BIOLOGY

Council of Biology Editors. *Scientific Style and Format: The CBE Manual for Authors, Editors, and Publishers.* 6th ed. New York: Cambridge UP, 1994.

BUSINESS

American Management Association. *The AMA Style Guide for Business Writing.* New York: AMACOM, 1996.

CHEMISTRY

Dodd, Janet S., ed. *The ACS Style Guide: A Manual for Authors and Editors.* Washington: Amer. Chemical Soc., 1986.

ENGLISH AND THE HUMANITIES (See section 31.)

Gibaldi, Joseph. *MLA Handbook for Writers of Research Papers.* 5th ed. New York: MLA, 1999.

GEOLOGY

Bates, Robert L., Rex Buchanan, and Marla Adkins-Heljeson, eds. *Geowriting: A Guide to Writing, Editing, and Printing in Earth Science.* 5th ed. Alexandria: Amer. Geological Inst., 1992.

GOVERNMENT DOCUMENTS

Garner, Diane L. *The Complete Guide to Citing Government Information Resources: A Manual for Writers and Librarians.* Rev. ed. Bethesda: Congressional Information Service, 1993.

United States Government Printing Office. *Manual of Style.* Washington: GPO, 1988.

HISTORY (See section 41.)

The Chicago Manual of Style. 14th ed. Chicago: U of Chicago P, 1993.

JOURNALISM

Goldstein, Norm, ed. *Associated Press Stylebook and Libel Manual.* 32nd ed. New York: Associated Press, 1997.

LAW

Columbia Law Review. *A Uniform System of Citation.* 16th ed. Cambridge: Harvard Law Rev. Assn., 1996.

LINGUISTICS

Linguistic Society of America. "LSA Style Sheet." Published annually in the December issue of the *LSA Bulletin.*

MATHEMATICS

American Mathematical Society. *The AMS Author Handbook: General Instructions for Preparing Manuscripts.* Providence: AMS, 1994.

MEDICINE

Iverson, Cheryl, et al. *American Medical Association Manual of Style: A Guide for Authors and Editors.* 9th ed. Baltimore: Williams, 1998.

MUSIC

Holoman, D. Kern, ed. *Writing about Music: A Style Sheet from the Editors of* 19th-Century Music. Berkeley: U of California P, 1988.

PHYSICS

American Institute of Physics. *Style Manual: Instructions to Authors and Volume Editors for the Preparation of AIP Book Manuscripts.* 5th ed. New York: AIP, 1995.

POLITICAL SCIENCE

American Political Science Association. *Style Manual for Political Science.* Rev. ed. Washington: Amer. Political Science Assn., 1993.

PSYCHOLOGY AND THE SOCIAL SCIENCES (See section 36.)

American Psychological Association. *Publication Manual of the American Psychological Association.* 5th ed. Washington: APA, 2001.

SCIENCE AND TECHNICAL WRITING

American National Standard for the Preparation of Scientific Papers for Written or Oral Presentation. New York: Amer. Natl. Standards Inst., 1979.

Microsoft Corporation. *Microsoft Manual of Style for Technical Publications.* Redmond, WA: Microsoft, 1998.

Rubens, Philip, ed. *Science and Technical Writing: A Manual of Style.* New York: Holt, 1992.

SOCIAL WORK

National Association of Social Workers. *Writing for NASW.* 2nd ed. Silver Springs: Natl. Assn. of Social Workers, 1994.

A Writer's Online Resources

Reference Sites

WWWebster Dictionary
< http://www.m-w.com/netdict.htm >

A Web of On-line Dictionaries
< http://www.facstaff.bucknell.edu/rbeard/
  diction.html >

OneLook Dictionaries
< http://www.onelook.com >

*ARTFL Project: Roget's Thesaurus Search
Form*
< http://humanities.uchicago.edu/
  forms_unrest/ROGET.html >

Atlapedia Online
< http://www.atlapedia.com >

Encyclopedia Smithsonian
< http://www.si.edu/resource/faq >

Writing Labs

Online Writery
< http://www.missouri.edu/~writery >

Purdue University Online Writing Lab
< http://owl.english.purdue.edu >

*The University of Michigan OWL: Online
Writing and Learning*
< http://www.lsa.umich.edu/ecb/help/owl.html >

ESL Sites

Dave's ESL Café
< http://eslcafe.com >

*Topics: An Online Magazine by and for
Learners of English*
< http://www.rice.edu/projects/topics/
  Electronic/Magazine.html >

Virtual Libraries

The Internet Public Library
< http://ipl.org >

The WWW Virtual Library
< http://vlib.org >

The Library of Congress
< http://lcweb.loc.gov >

Thor: Purdue University Libraries
< http://thorplus.lib.purdue.edu/index.html >

The Webliography: Internet Subject Guides
< http://www.lib.lsu.edu/weblio.html >

Text Archives

Electronic Text Center — University of Virginia Library
< http://etext.lib.virginia.edu >

Project Bartleby Archive
< http://www.columbia.edu/acis/bartleby >

Project Gutenberg
< http://promo.net/pg >

Government Sites

U.S. Census Bureau: The Official Statistics
< http://www.census.gov >

Thomas: Legislative Information on the Internet
< http://thomas.loc.gov >

U.S. State & Local Gateway
< http://www.statelocal.gov >

U.S. Government Printing Office
< http://www.access.gpo.gov >

United Nations
< http://www.un.org >

News Sites

The New York Times on the Web
< http://www.nytimes.com >

The Washington Post
< http://www.washingtonpost.com >

U.S. News Online
< http://www.usnews.com/usnews/home.htm >

nationalgeographic.com
< http://www.nationalgeographic.com/main.html >

CNN Interactive
< http://www.cnn.com >

Newsgroups and Listservs

Tile.Net
< http://www.tile.net >

Liszt
< http://www.liszt.com >

Deja News
< http://www.dejanews.com >

Bedford/St. Martin's Sites

Hacker Handbook Home Page
< http://www.bedfordstmartins.com/hacker >

Research and Documentation Online (links to sites in a variety of disciplines)
< http://www.bedfordstmartins.com/hacker/resdoc >

Bedford Links to Resources in Literature
< http://www.bedfordstmartins.com/litlinks >

Bedford/St. Martin's Links to History Resources
< http://www.bedfordstmartins.com/history/
historylinks.html >

Sites for Evaluating Sources

"Checklist for Evaluating Web Sites,"
Canisius College Library & Internet
< http://www.canisius.edu/canhp/canlib/
webcrit.htm >

"Evaluating Web Sites: Criteria and Tools,"
Olin Kroch Uris Libraries
< http://www.library.cornell.edu/okuref/research/
webeval.html >

"Evaluating Internet Information," *Internet Navigator*
< http://sol.slcc.edu/lr/navigator/discovery/
eval.html >

Index

Checklist for Global Revisions

Focus

▶ Is the thesis stated clearly enough?
  Is it placed where readers will notice it?
▶ Does each idea support the thesis?

Organization

▶ Can readers easily follow the structure?
  Would headings help?
▶ Do topic sentences signal new ideas?
▶ Are ideas presented in a logical order?

Content

▶ Is the supporting material persuasive?
▶ Are important ideas fully developed?
▶ Is the draft concise enough — free of irrelevant
  or repetitious material?
▶ Are the parts proportioned sensibly?
  Do major ideas receive enough attention?

Style

▶ Is the voice appropriate — not too stuffy, not
  too breezy?
▶ Are the sentences clear, emphatic, and varied?

Use of Quotations

▶ Is quoted material introduced with a signal
  phrase and documented with a citation?
▶ Is quoted material enclosed within quotation
  marks (unless it has been set off from the text)?
▶ Is each quotation word-for-word accurate?
  If not, do brackets or ellipsis dots mark the
  changes or omissions?

Use of Other Source Material

▶ Is the draft free of plagiarism? Are summaries
  and paraphrases written in the writer's own
  words — not copied or half-copied from the
  source?
▶ Has source material that is not common
  knowledge been documented?

Revision Symbols

abbr	abbreviation **23a**		" "	quotation marks **20**
ad	adverb or adjective **13**		.	period **21a**
add	add needed word **4**		?	question mark **21b**
agr	agreement **10, 12a**		!	exclamation point **21c**
appr	inappropriate language **9**		—	dash **21d**
art	article **16a**		( )	parentheses **21e**
awk	awkward		[ ]	brackets **21f**
cap	capital letter **22**		. . .	ellipsis mark **21g**
case	case **12c, 12d**		/	slash **21h**
cs	comma splice **15**		*pass*	ineffective passive **2, 11d**
dm	dangling modifier **7c**		*pn agr*	pronoun agreement **12a**
-ed	*-ed* ending **11a**		*ref*	pronoun reference **12b**
ESL	English as a second language **16**		*run-on*	run-on sentence **15**
frag	sentence fragment **14**		*-s*	*-s* ending on verb **10, 16b**
fs	fused sentence **15**		*sexist*	sexist language **9c, 12a**
hyph	hyphen **24b**		*shift*	confusing shift **5**
irreg	irregular verb **11a**		*sl*	slang **9b**
ital	italics (underlining) **23c**		*sp*	misspelled word **24a**
jarg	jargon **9a**		*sv agr*	subject-verb agreement **10**
lc	use lowercase letter **22**		*t*	verb tense **11b**
mix	mixed construction **6**		*usage*	see Glossary of Usage
mm	misplaced modifier **7a–b, 7d**		*v*	voice **2, 11d**
mood	mood **11c**		*var*	sentence variety **8**
num	numbers **23b**		*vb*	problem with verb **11, 16b–c**
om	omitted word **4, 16a, 16c**		*w*	wordy **1**
	punctuation		//	faulty parallelism **3**
	comma **17a–i**		^	insert
no ,	no comma **17j**		x	obvious error
	semicolon **18a**		#	insert space
	colon **18b**		⌒	close up space
	apostrophe **19**			

Contents